2.99

AFTER SHOCK

TED KITCHENS

AFTER SHOCK

What to Do *When Leaders* (and others) *Fail You*

MULTNOMAH

Portland, Oregon

Unless otherwise indicated, all Scripture references are from the Holy Bible: New International Version, c 1973, 1978, 1984 by the International Bible Society. Used by permission of Zondervan Bible Publishers.

Edited by Rodney L. Morris
Cover design by Bruce DeRoos

AFTERSHOCK
© 1992 by Ted Kitchens
Published by Multnomah Press
10209 SE Division Street
Portland, Oregon 97266

Multnomah Press is a ministry of
Multnomah School of the Bible
8435 NE Glisan Street
Portland, Oregon 97220

Printed in the United States of America.

Library of Congress Cataloging-in-Publication Data

Kitchens, Ted.
    Aftershock : what to do when leaders (and others) fail you / Ted Kitchens
        p.   cm.
    ISBN 0-88070-423-3
    1. Christian leadership. 2. Clergy—Conduct of life.
3. Christian life—1960-   I. Title.
BV652.1.K58 1992
262'.1—dc20   92-10004
                                                         CIP

92 93 94 95 96 97 98 99 00 01 - 10 9 8 7 6 5 4 3 2 1

Dedication

This book is affectionately dedicated
to my dearest friends and fellow believers
at Christ Chapel Bible Church
in Fort Worth, Texas.
Their love for me, their encouragement,
their authenticity, and their integrity for Christ
has motivated me to continue
to run the race to win the prize.

Contents

Foreword

He was a man's man, a former All-American football player who had gone through one of the finest seminaries in the country. Now as the regional director of a ministry, I (John) was closely involved with him as a student, he was the first man to truly disciple and train me.

I look up to this man and prayed I could be like him. I'd mow his yard just to be around him, and we spent hours fishing, talking about the future, and praying. In many ways, I loved him as the father I never had growing up in a single-parent home. Perhaps that's why I walked in the rain for hours, crying my eyes out, on the day I heard he had fallen.

Not him. Not the one person who I thought of all others would go to the wall honoring and upholding Christ's name. And while I hated to admit it, the same tremor that shattered his ministry and family also shook my faith as well.

I wish I would have had Ted Kitchens's book in my hands back then. I needed to understand how the cracks could have formed in my friend's life. I longed to know how to respond, both personally and to my fallen friend. I ached to know what to do with my colliding emotions, and to realize that someone else knew and understood my pain. And perhaps most of all, I wanted to know what to do to help my own pastor keep from stumbling in the future and experiencing all that hurt over again.

There are many books we all should read. But this is

a book we must read. With Satan's strategy of going after Christian leaders today, we need the biblical insight and practical wisdom offered in *Aftershock*.

Don't worry. While this book will help us deal with men and women who have failed, it isn't written in mud for "Geraldo" or the *National Enquirer*. Dr. Kitchens's compassion, sensitivity, and desire for restoration the biblical way keeps the focus where it should be—on Christ and on what a godly response to failure ought to be. And in a clear, easily readable way, he lays out a plan of action to deal with and avoid failure that every church, and every member sitting in church, should be practicing.

If you're one of the 1 percent who has never been disappointed by a Christian friend or leader, then you don't need this book. But for the rest of us who have felt that stabbing pain of betrayal, and who feel shame for what is happening to the name of Christ today, this excellent book is an answer to prayer.

Gary Smalley
John Trent

Acknowledgments

This book was a concert of love played by many. I want to gratefully thank the following people for helping make it a reality:

My wife, Lynn: The spirit of purity for Christ lives in this book and in your love for Him. Thank you for the confidence you gave me and for the many mornings and evenings we were absent from each other. You're the most valuable player of all.

John Trent: For encouragement unlimited! Thanks for the hours on the telephone and in the airports. You are my friend.

Tim Kimmel: For the zeal you bring to the art of writing and the wisdom you gave me on this project.

Sharon Wimberly: Who typed thousands of pages and slaved over unending details because you believe in me.

Chad Winsor, Billie Hara, Jack Norris, and Ray Carter: Your role of reading and critiquing the manuscript was a labor of love.

Rod Morris: Multnomah is blessed to have you as a senior editor. You are superb at your trade and a man of grace, wisdom, and kindness. Thank you for the way you treated me.

Kassie and Tyler: For being the most understanding children a father can have. All right, all right kids . . . now Dad can come out and play!

Introduction

They hadn't even sung the "Star Spangled Banner."
It began with a rumble that sounded like the thunder of
fans' feet. The light towers about the stadium began to
rock back and forth. The outfield rolled like an ocean.
Players scurried onto the field followed by a swarm of
police. The upper deck began to jettison concrete frag-
ments onto the thousands below.

Twenty-five minutes from the first fastball, the 1989
World Series "Battle of the Bays" was becoming the
"Rattle of the Bays."[1] Most of the almost sixty thousand
expectant fans at Candlestick Park reacted to the earthquake in a "stunned, uneasy silence."[2]

The Richter registered 6.9 at 5:04 P.M. on October 17,
1989, shaking the third game of the World Series and the
San Francisco Bay area to its foundation. The war of the
plates raged not on the diamond but under the city. In a
matter of thirty seconds, without warning, lives were
changed and rearranged. Some would take years to
rebuild; others would never be the same.

They hadn't even sung the final doxology. The chair-
man of the elder board approached the pulpit. He bowed
his salt-and-pepper head of hair for a silent moment. He
needed composure. The pews were filled with good people
who had put their trust in a fallen pastor. A few knew the
truth the rest would soon learn. When he lifted his head
and began to read the prepared statement, the lights overhead reflected the tears tracking down his cheeks. Within
thirty seconds, the congregation was sitting in stunned,

uneasy silence. Without warning, their lives had been rearranged by a shifting human faultline. The lives of some in the congregation would take years to rebuild; others would never be the same.

Below the surface of every Christian's life there exists great potential for a spiritual quake. Within each believer, opposing forces are at work pushing in opposite directions. At this epicenter, the Holy Spirit pushes for devotion, commitment, and faithfulness against the world and the natural pressure of pride, lust, and greed. If the pressure along this human faultline builds and sin occurs, this slippage can cause shockwaves and cracks that open and swallow other believers up and down the Kingdom of Christ. It doesn't matter what the Christian's spiritual position, dangerous pressure causing cracks and faultlines exists within.

The church, the community, and the world can feel the shaking effects of spiritual fissure. Never has the body of Christ experienced more private failure producing such public shame. The last ten years have brought the integrity of Christianity to its knees. The Christian community has become painfully aware that there is an active faultline that can change lives in seconds.

The media is ever hungry for a scoop on the latest Christian to fall. Headlines from the last few years splatter the shame on our doorstep:

CHURCH MEMBER ADMITS SIN,
LEAVES COMMUNITY

CONFESSION PROMPTS
GASPS AND TEARS

CHURCH CLOSES . . .
MINISTER DEFROCKED
LEADER DECLARES VICTORY OVER
DEMON OF LUST
PASTOR ASKS WIFE FOR FORGIVENESS

In black and white we are constantly reminded that the bride of Christ is sullied and is staggering from her self-inflicted moral wounds.

In the four years I have spent researching and preparing this work, I have experienced embarrassment for the church, fatigue from helping those hurt, and fear because I don't want my feet of clay to crumble. While striving to save the integrity of my work and those around me, I have personally witnessed the fall of:

twenty Christian couples
ten pastors
two seminary professors
three local leaders
two national leaders

Let me pull two examples out of my files.

Jerry was struggling as a second-year student in a Christian school. He and his wife, Valerie, had not anticipated the stress of being away from their family and friends and at the same time straining to pay the high cost of education. They lived in a small garage apartment. They bought food only when it was on sale. With the long nights of study and the grinding days of classwork and mechanic duties at the local garage, Jerry and Valerie began to resent each other. In desperation they sought counseling help at the school.

The counselor was kind and understanding and free.

Throughout their many appointments, Jerry held high hopes for the rebuilding of a floundering marriage. He thought, "By Thanksgiving, our love will be back together." When Thanksgiving arrived, Jerry found himself alone in his dark study trying to piece his life back together, embracing only despair. Valerie was in another state . . . embracing their Christian counselor! The young couple and the believing community were devastated; the faultline widened.

In her book, *Survivor of a Tarnished Ministry*, Betty Esses illustrates this shocking truth in the life of her husband, a popular minister and author who began to live a secretly sordid masquerade.[3] Even though, in Betty's own words, "he has an impeccable public image throughout his ministry, he lied about both his ordination and his theological credentials. For the twenty-eight years that we were married, he was unfaithful to me each year during his ministry." He pilfered over $100,000 from the offering plate at the same time he was writing a bestselling book. Mrs. Esses's ex-husband is still undiscovered as he pastors a large congregation in another state.

The soft glow of stained glass and the perfume of fresh roses can mislead. Behind the trappings of evangelicalism there are pews and pulpits filled with Christians poised for a plunge into pain.

Even though Christian leaders make the front page of the *National Enquirer* or the lead interview on "Nightline," many of us can remain detached. A well-known leader's fall does not undermine our relationship with God. The TV anchorman might make them squirm in their hypocritical seats, but we're simply spectators.

It's different when it's the man or woman in the center frame of my life. It's different when it's the man or woman we put more confidence in than anyone else. When it's my closest friend, my pastor, my choir director, my youth pastor or Sunday school teacher, the betrayal shakes the foundation of my faith. That which was one day solid, reliable, and trustworthy can crack without warning, becoming an emotional crevice.

I have noticed a trend. Satan has found that the best way to scatter the sheep is to attack the weak and then assault the shepherds. In the chapters ahead, we will consider principles for keeping our Christian testimony true and answer these pressing questions:

- Why are so many Christians tainting the honor of God today?
- What first-century formula has the church today overlooked that can return her strength, power, and effectiveness?
- How can a fractured Christian rebuild his life?
- How can I protect myself from disappointing others?
- How can the church prevent future cracks in its integrity?
- How can I faultproof my pastors or spiritual leaders?
- How should the church restore a fallen shepherd?

The problems are complex, but the solutions are not. The surgery that must be performed will not be without pain. We'd love to be anesthetized beforehand, but moral infection must be treated when we're wide awake and all our senses are on call to respond. The solutions may not be painless, but they exist right in the heart of every church; we have merely failed to see them. The first-century family of God had a spiritual tool box that was used to prevent such moral contamination. Tools the body of Christ today desperately needs to put back into use.

Our Focus

I want to offer you more than information. I want to give you hope and the ability to believe again. The pages ahead were written to answer questions, salve wounds, and save the fallen. We can have confidence regardless of what has happened in the past or what we may encounter in the future.

You will be given practical steps for fault-proofing yourself, your Christian friends, and your spiritual leaders. You will discover a simple thermometer to evaluate your fellowship's weakness. Together, we will peer over the edge, into the darkness of the faultline. When we get a better grip on the edge and learn from God, we will see his light shine through that bleak hole of our moral failure.

In these turbulent times, *Aftershock* is a biblical blueprint for rebuilding the integrity of the most significant force on earth: the body of Christ.

Notes

1. Jim Reeves, "Thirty Seconds of Terror and Nowhere to Run," *Star Telegram* (Fort Worth), 18 October 1989, 1.

2. Steve Campbell, "No Bayball Game," *Star Telegram* (Fort Worth), 18 October 1989, 7.

3. Betty Esses DeBlase, *Survivor of a Tarnished Ministry: The True Story of Michael and Betty Esses* (Orange, Calif.: Truth Publishers, Inc. 1983).

PART ONE

Victims of a Tremor

CHAPTER ONE

The Cracks of Our Times:
Living in the "Gimme" Generation

Recently, a smiling young couple from California presented me with an unusual gift. It was a brightly-colored T-shirt. On the front of the shirt is a map of the West Coast, featuring all the geological faults in brilliant streaks of red. Directly below, in large, bold letters, it declares, "California has its faults." Within the humor of these words lies the seriousness of the ever-present danger in that part of our country.

I've since thought that some aggressive, entrepreneurial Christian might do well if he produced a similar T-shirt, one that proclaims on the front, "Christians have their faults . . ." and on the back, "and I fell in one." It's a fact of life. Christians make mistakes. These days it is especially apparent that the bride of Christ is wearing a soiled dress.

Widening Crevices

When the guard closed the steel door on Gary, he stood, head against the cold gray bars, and wept. The judge had dropped the gavel and sentenced this young man to grow old apart from his family. But Gary is no ordinary convict. He was a conscientious, godly man who raised a wonderful family. He was voted "most likely to succeed" in his college class. He was endowed with impressive gifts as a pastor.

But compromise sneaked into his pastor's study. Over the course of several years, his counseling ministry became more and more demanding, and he became more and more manipulative. Pressure along the faultline built to the breaking point. The result was a major tremor. Gary was guilty of assaulting and molesting four of his counselees, a disastrous move that claimed five families. A whole church collapsed in the aftershock of another Christian leader on the faultline.

Yet often those who hurt us are not our spiritual leaders. An influential Christian in our life could cause this same heartache: unethical actions within a Christian business, the moral collapse of a believing friend, a trust betrayed, rejection, physical or verbal abuse. The result is the same. Hurt can leave us reeling in the effects of aftershock. When a Christian we admire says no to moral compromise, only to announce by his actions that he can no longer uphold such a high standard, that's a hard hit for any of us to endure. These are all cracks of our times.

But before passing too harsh a judgment on the epidemic of moral laxity in the body, we need to focus on the escalating problem. Why are we allowing it to get worse? What attitudes are resident within the Christian community that actually attract this embarrassment?

1. ABSORBED BY SELF

Preach the Word; be prepared in season and out of season; correct, rebuke and encourage—with great patience and careful instruction. For the time will come when men will not put up with sound doctrine. Instead, to suit their own desires, they will gather around them a great number of teachers to say what their itching ears want to hear. They will turn their ears away from the truth and turn aside to myths (2 Tim. 4:2-4).

At times, the media sees the causes of many of our struggles more clearly than most Christians do. The *Wall Street Journal* recently carried an unbelievable story about the gullibility of some Christians. How is it that the members of one Sunday school class could allow a man who claims to be led by God to entice them into investing their life savings in bogus scams? *The Journal* explains the problem by tagging our society "the gimme generation."

Tragically, many Christians have slipped into this "give-me" mode. They have a passion for their personal goals more than for the things of God. Anytime God's people are consumed by self-centeredness, heartaches are inevitable.

A Card-Carrying Member

As soon as I gave the benediction and stepped down from the pulpit, Joel came out of the crowd. He was a twenty-eight-year-old hairstylist, fashionably dressed and carrying a new Bible. His introduction and smile put me at ease. He was likable and energetic. During our short conversation, several terms Joel used signaled me that he was young in the faith, with a warped view of God. He was a card-carrying member of the "gimme" generation.

His questions tipped me off. He was in big-time financial trouble, and he wanted help from me and God. I could tell that getting ahead was a high priority to this new friend.

During the week, I couldn't get Joel off my mind. I sent him a book from my library, sure that he would benefit from reading it. Then we scheduled a meeting for lunch. Over a bowl of soup, this young man shared the careless and exorbitant way he mishandled his income. Over lunch, I shared with Joel the teaching of 1 Timothy 6:6-10, concluding with the verse, "Some people, eager for money, have wandered from the faith and pierced themselves with many griefs."

I put two questions to Joel: "Would you be willing to serve Christ even if it means living in poverty for the rest of your life?" and, "Joel, are you devoted to Christ because of who he is, or for what you think he can give you?"

The power of self-interest should not be underestimated. Joel has never returned to our fellowship.

The Divine Slot Machine

Joel is only one sad example of the self-absorbed Christian caught up in the "health, wealth, and prosperity" gospel. He saw God as his personal treasure chest, a divine money machine. Unfortunately, many Christians give not out of joy or obedience but in order to get. Even though the New Testament does promise both spiritual and financial provisions for those who obediently give, God promises his involvement in our *needs*, not our selfish *wants* (2 Cor. 9:6-8). God is not a holy slot machine waiting to spill out heavenly coins. The "give to get" mentality is a clear indicator that we are living in a selfish generation. Delayed gratification is seldom practiced. It's an ominous sign of the times.

Blinded by Success

The self-centered Christian has a distorted view of success. Success is defined by outward appearances, positions, and possessions. The life God has called us to lead cannot be attained when evaluating our lives through such worldly themes. It is critical that we define success using God's definition rather than man's. What is God's idea of success?

> Do not let this Book of the Law depart from your mouth; meditate on it day and night, so that you may be careful to do everything written in it. Then you will be prosperous and successful (Josh. 1:8).
>
> Blessed is the man
>   who does not walk in the counsel of the wicked
> or stand in the way of sinners
>   or sit in the seat of mockers.
> But his delight is in the law of the LORD,
>   and on his law he meditates day and night.
> He is like a tree planted by streams of water,
>   which yields its fruit in season
> and whose leaf does not wither.
>   Whatever he does prospers (Psa. 1:1-3).

Believing that God *does* desire our success, how should we define success in biblical terms? Ron Jensen writes, "Biblical success is the progressive realization and internalization of all that God wants me to be and do."[1] Success is first "being," then out of Christian character will come forth the "doing." In the Kingdom of God, success is pleasing our Heavenly Father and relying upon him for our daily provisions. Matthew 6:33 tells us, "But seek first his kingdom and his righteousness, and all these things will be given to you as well."

The inward focus on "me" has given rise to a new definition of success in the church. We're no longer asking ourselves the right questions:

* "Is there humility and holiness in my life and in the lives of those in my church?"
* "Do we operate with ethical principles and moral purity?"
* "Are we preaching the unfailing riches of the cross of Christ without compromise?"

Neglecting God's principles of success can mislead the churchgoer as well as the church leader into the false assumption that God is solely concerned with outward appearances. In these cases, pragmatism may win over God's truth. Church leaders may focus on irrelevant issues which please the ears of believers who desire to live selfish lives.

The material goals of life have silently placed a pillow over the face of spiritual goals and smothered them to death. It has become difficult to distinguish the church from the nonbelieving world. No wonder the call to holiness is only a faint voice easily ignored.

2. ATTRACTED TO THE COUNTERFEITS

Watch out for false prophets. They come to you in sheep's clothing, but inwardly they are ferocious wolves (Matt. 7:15).

I've always been impressed with how the FBI trains its new agents to spot counterfeit currency. The trainers do just the opposite of what I would expect. Instead of locking the new recruits in a room to study piles of phony bills, they first acquaint the men with genuine, hot off the press, grade A, government issue greenbacks. Learning what the genuine looks like keeps the agent from being duped and our country from being overtaken with bad currency.

In a similar way, if we are to avoid living counterfeit lives—or being led by counterfeits—we must become experts in identifying men and ministries that have the genuine mark of God's character on them. In a society enveloped in success and self, this is no easy task.

Along a major highway leading into one of the largest cities in the South stands an enormous billboard promoting the ministry of a well-known televangelist. The promises made and the claims projected on this huge road sign are enough to cause a discerning Christian to wonder. The most shocking aspect of the billboard is the gigantic picture of the evangelist's smiling face. There is something about his self-promotion that should disturb every believer.

I know that God does use the media to reach people with the gospel, so I decided to tune in the evangelist's daily television program. I wanted to be open-minded, but not once was I able to reconcile his strange doctrines with the basic truths of the New Testament. He was a counterfeit.

Recently I picked up a newspaper from that city and read a front-page story on an extravaganza this ministry held. Over eight thousand people had crowded into the convention hall wanting their itching ears to be scratched. I suspect that one of the faces in the crowd was my friend Joel.

Lining Up to Be Deceived

I have great respect for the many godly evangelists and pastors who follow our Lord's calling; however, the front pages of our newspapers have been pointing out for years that the church has too many phonies. I recently clipped this item from a magazine. It is a metaphor of our times.

> A man observed a fellow driving a group of sheep across a field, beating the stick and urging them forward. "I thought shepherds led their sheep," said the man. The answer came back: "I'm not the shepherd; I'm the butcher."[2]

A noted expert on cults sadly informed me that Christians are currently "lining up by the thousands to be deceived." The false teaching is subtly different from the genuine article, demanding that a believer be fully dedicated to Christ and steeped in the truth in order to spot deceivers. One writer sees the problem clearly:

> Satan will use any approach to keep us from experiencing the full measure of God's riches. Any error, no matter how small or great, will do. He works through the current world philosophies, through Bible verses taken out of context, through charismatic personalities who "sound" so right and sincere. No method is overlooked in Satan's attempt to mislead the chosen of God.
>
> *Satan says*: Seek success at any price.
>
> *God says*: "But seek first His kingdom and His righteousness; and all these things shall be added to you" (Matthew 6:33).
>
> *Satan says*: Seek riches at any cost.

God says: "Do not lay up for yourselves treasures on earth. . . . But lay up for yourselves treasures in heaven" (Matthew 6:19, 20).

Satan says: Be popular; push ahead.

God says: "If anyone wishes to come after Me, let him deny himself . . ." (Matthew 16:24).

Satan says: If you don't look after yourself, no one else will. God helps those who help themselves.

God says: "Do nothing from selfishness or empty conceit, but with humility of mind let each of you regard one another as more important than himself" (Philippians 2:3,4).

Satan says: I can't be happy unless I'm married (or: I can't be happy unless I'm out of this marriage).

God says: "I have learned to be content in whatever circumstances I am" (Philippians 4:11).

Satan says: Eat, drink, and be merry, for tomorrow we die.

God says: "Man does not live by bread alone, but on every word that comes from the mouth of God" (Matthew 4:4).

Satan says: If it feels good, do it.

God says: "Not my will, but Thine be done" (Luke 22:42).

Satan says: Everything is relative.

God says: "Thy Word is truth" (John 17:17).[3]

The plumb line for life, the only way to spot what is off center in an age like ours, is to know what the real thing looks like and then to be real ourselves.

Back to the Book

This cannot be accomplished unless we are a people of the Book. Only God's Word supplies truth to a heart prone to selfish wanderings. It takes careful study of a roadmap to place a lost driver back on the right course. Likewise, a Christian can expect to be stranded on a winding road of confusion apart from the guiding truth of God's Word. That's why Paul warns Timothy, "Preach the Word." It is a safeguard against selfish living and a healing salve to those who have been wounded by counterfeits.

3. ABSENCE OF ACCOUNTABILITY

Let the Word of Christ dwell in you richly as you teach and admonish one another with all wisdom, and as you sing psalms, hymns and spiritual songs with gratitude in your hearts to God (Col. 3:16).

Submit to one another out of reverence for Christ (Eph. 5:21).

Therefore confess your sins to each other and pray for each other (James 5:16a).

As Christians walk higher and higher on the high wire of responsibility and authority, they must take precaution to balance their lives and ministry against the gusty winds of personal imbalance. The Word of God tells us that we have an enemy on the outside pushing against us (1 Pet. 5:8) while at the same time we struggle with sin at work within (Rom. 7:21). Regardless of your vocation or your station in life, a warning from Paul should be burned into your memory, "If you think you are standing firm, be careful that you don't fall!" (1 Cor. 10:12).

Every Christian leader and layperson needs a balancing rod that will keep everything in perspective. One side of the balance is inner character; the other side is outer accountability. When the winds of temptation gust, these two can be called into use to keep believers from a deadly fall.

The Christian life necessitates the involvement of other caring Christian brothers and sisters. Someone must be asking the tough questions: "What are some of your inner struggles?" "Where are you spending your idle time?" "How is your private time with the Lord?" "How can I be praying for you?" "How are you doing in your personal prayer and study of God's Word?" It is essential for someone to be touching these hidden areas of our lives so we do not lose our balance.

One newspaper reporter records her observations about a ministry that lacked accountability:

> In a sense, the televangelist's resort seemed shattered as any coastal town blasted by a severe hurricane. Sure, lawns were clipped, signs painted. But there was a depressed stillness. The heart of the place had been torn out. An abandoned crane loomed over the boarded-up, 21-story Tower Hotel, a monument to the evangelists's greed. He conned listeners into donating 66 million dollars to the 24 million dollar project, then left the hotel a dying hulk. At the next-door Grand Hotel, ghostly hymn music piped into the lobby hung with paintings of Christ. A crude sign said, "$49 a night for four." The desk clerk said the hotel was 20% occupied. Hard to believe. Field mice, the wind and Catawba Indians will inherit it. Maybe somebody will erect a sign: "The Wages of sin . . ."[4]

The cause of the devastation: authority without accountability.

Consider the fall of King David. We have no proof that David had anyone in his kingdom addressing the issue of power in his life. A tragedy! Not only was David not under any apparent accountability, he was virtually living in isolation from others. Success pushed David further away from intimacy and accountable relationships. He abandoned his values and slipped into murder and adultery.

The Christian faith is a relational faith. We are a family. We need to hold each other accountable to our Christian responsibilities by honestly involving ourselves in others' lives. This takes time and energy. This takes love.

4. ABANDONED BIBLICAL BLUEPRINT

There is a fourth reason Christians have allowed the church's testimony to suffer so much over the past few years. The unique blueprint that Christ gave the church to maintain her purity has been abandoned. This blueprint empowered the early church to minister effectively to the self-indulgent brother or sister, or the one living a rebellious life. It is a purity plan that the church must return to if spiritual health is to be restored. As long as the sheep refuse to use the biblical methods that Christ himself gave, spiritual tremors will continue to shake the body of Christ.

Before I reveal the blueprint, I'm convinced many Christians are not aware of the corporate damage being done by each moral failure in the church. While many Christians understand the personal damage of anger, grief, doubt, lost trust, and spiritual apathy, few understand the corporate devastation that can result. Our spiritual violations affect not only us, they also affect others—some we have never known or met. The following chapter uncovers four hidden dangers of this aftershock.

Notes

1. Ron Jensen, *How to Succeed the Biblical Way* (Wheaton, Ill.: Tyndale House Publishers, 1983), 12.

2. *Preaching*, Jan-Feb 1987, 52.

3. *Satan Says—God Says*, source unknown.

4. Sandy Grady, "Hugo and Tammy," *Star Telegram* (Fort Worth), 23 September 1989, Sec. 1, 29.

CHAPTER TWO

_____

The Ripple Effect:
A Principle of Corporate Solidarity

The eruption of Mount St. Helens in Washington State in May of 1980 is certain to be remembered as one of the most significant geologic events of the twentieth century. The explosion was initiated by an earthquake and rockslide involving one-half cubic mile of rock. The explosion released energy equivalent to 20 million tons of TNT, which toppled 150 square miles of forest in six minutes. In Spirit Lake, just north of the volcano, an enormous wave of water, initiated by one-eighth cubic mile of rockslide debris, stripped trees from slopes as high as 850 feet above the pre-eruption water level. The total energy output was equivalent to 400 million tons of TNT—approximately 20,000 Hiroshima-size atomic bombs.[1]

A few miles from the eruption, a small band of

Christian women made camp in a peaceful valley by a rambling brook. One moment, their biggest concern was washing the soap from their hair in the cool mountain stream; the next moment they were facing a bone-crushing wall of water. All but two were slammed to their deaths beneath a tidal wave of rock, foliage, and mud.

In Spokane, two hundred miles to the east, one of my staff members was engaged in a testy game of tennis. Interrupted by a panicked passerby, the tennis duo was warned to "run for your life." By midafternoon, the sky had blackened and given up a great snow of ash. The next morning, Spokane was blanketed with one-and-a-half inches of fine gray powder. The eruption of Mount St. Helens had left its mark far from the actual explosion.

When Christians fail, the effect is felt both near and far. Whether the impact is like that of a bursting dam washing away those closest to it or of a suffocating ash blanketing a wider area, the damage is real.

A Hurting Reality

What aftershocks do we experience when someone falls or commits an act that violates another? After watching the Christian community's response to the casualties, I'm convinced we do not understand how badly it hurts.

I felt it a few weeks ago at a Bible study. There are fifteen members in the group from every walk of life and maturity level. That night I asked: "Has a friend or Christian leader ever disappointed you and broken your heart?"

I was not prepared for the explosion of anger and hurt. All but one let their emotions fly. One of the men painfully remembered, "It hurts just to talk about it." Pent-up hurt poured out from deep within their wounded hearts.

In my fifteen years of ministry, I've observed a spiritual phenomenon that always occurs when God's people are disobedient. I call it the "ripple effect." Similar to the Mount St. Helens eruption, when sin erupts in and around our lives, it establishes a pattern of consequences or fallout that ripples from the point of eruption out toward other people of God. When sin erupts in the life of a believer, the consequences are never isolated; they reach out and touch most of those around.

This principle is illustrated throughout biblical history, but one of the more memorable examples occurred during the time of Joshua, the great commander of the Lord's army. Every time I read the biblical account, it gets my full attention.

Learning from History

The scene opens in chapter 6 of the book of Joshua. What a wondrous time in the history of the Jewish nation! The Israelites marched confidently around Jericho, and God's foot supernaturally toppled the fortress walls. For the sake of purity, God's people were instructed to touch nothing and take nothing from the valuable ruins of Jericho. All possessions of the city were "banned."

> But keep away from the devoted things, so that you will not bring about your own destruction by taking any of them. Otherwise you will make the camp of Israel liable to destruction and bring trouble on it. All the silver and gold and the articles of bronze and iron are sacred to the LORD and must go into his treasury (Josh. 6:18-19).

Like so many of God's commands, this one did not go unbroken. Someone disobeyed and took from the crumbled ruins of Jericho some of the "off-limits" articles.

Chapter 7 opens with the nation anticipating another easy victory. Joshua's army surrounds its second target: the small town of Ai. The troops are so confident that Joshua dispatches only three thousand men. But to their shock, these mighty soldiers are pushed back and flee for their lives. That evening, the nation sits around the campfires in dismay and humiliation, while thirty-six families mourn the loss of loved ones (Josh. 7:4-9).

What a stunning reversal! In his confusion, Joshua humbled himself and sought the reason for Israel's devastating defeat. Then, God pointed his divine finger at the source of the eruption:

> The LORD said to Joshua, "Stand up! What are you doing down on your face? Israel has sinned; they have violated my covenant, which I commanded them to keep. They have taken some of the devoted things; they have stolen, they have lied, they have put them with their own possessions. That is why the Israelites cannot stand against their enemies; they turn their backs and run because they have been made liable to destruction. I will not be with you anymore unless you destroy whatever among you is devoted to destruction (Josh. 7:10-12).

One of the Israelites had disobeyed, causing a ripple of contamination that rained down on all the tribes of Israel.

The following day, Joshua was guided by God's hand to the contaminator; his name was Achan (Josh. 7:16-18). Joshua confronts Achan and a confession is made, but the penalty for his sin is stiff: Achan, his family, and his animals were stoned to death, then burned!

Why so harsh? The Word of God gives us four significant

principles concerning the consequences of sin that every believer needs to understand and live by each day of his Christian walk. Disobedience is serious business.

Principle 1: Disobedience Always Starts a Ripple Effect

> Israel has sinned; they have violated my covenant, which I commanded them to keep. They have taken some of the devoted things; they have stolen, they have lied, they have put them with their own possessions (Josh. 7:11).

Only Achan disobeyed God, yet God accuses the whole nation of violating his command. God believes in collective guilt. Achan's sin touched the lives of the entire people of God. It began with his family, moved out to the thirty-six families that lost husbands and fathers, and settled on the outer fringes of the camp.

This principle of corporate solidarity is far-reaching both personally and theologically. The sinful acts of one man can bring retribution and judgment to an entire believing family.

> The individual functions within the larger context of the community of which he is a part. Achan robbed the whole nation of the purity and holiness which it ought to possess before God.[2]

Starting a Ripple

Pete sat in my office chair, wringing his dark green tie and staring at his shoes. Over the next hour, he talked about three concerns in his life. He had lost his self-confidence; the new job he had so enthusiastically taken crumbled because of personality conflicts; and, most significantly, his relationship with his wife was stale and almost dead. Now she was suffering several new emotional and physical strains.

Throughout the hour, I had an uneasy spirit. Something wasn't right; something was hidden . . . out of sight. I silently prayed that God would give me counsel for Pete. Some way to help him. Pete and those his life touched were suffering from some problem that seemed to be hidden from everyone's view but God's.

At the end of the hour, we took time to be silent and contemplate. When the time seemed right, I prayed that Pete would not be offended, and said, "Pete, you're hiding something. You're not telling me the real source of your problems. Something is causing you and all those around you to suffer. Would you tell me what it is?"

After moments of silence, with embarrassment he answered, "You're right. I'm addicted to pornography. Somehow it's affecting everything in my life."

That hidden sin was causing a ripple, starting in his household, moving out to his work, and on to the very edges of his life. Finally, he had come to grips with the devastation of his secret sin.

The ripple effect of sin is underscored in the New Testament. We find it in Paul's letter to the church at Corinth where he preaches the truth that all Christians are a part of the whole body of Christ: "Now the body is not made up of one part but of many" (1 Cor. 12:14), and in verse 20, "there are many parts, but one body."

No Christian lives in isolation. We cannot deny that we are all together under one umbrella, but we overlook that Christians live as a corporate unit experiencing solidarity and oneness. This connectedness means, "If one part suffers, every part suffers with it; if one part is honored, every part rejoices with it" (v. 26). And if one member sins, in some way it affects the other members. Paul uses yeast to illustrate the ripple effect: "Don't you know that a little yeast works through the whole batch of dough?" (1 Cor. 5:6).

Transgression, like yeast, contaminates more than its own small corner of the loaf.

We are a body. Your activities this week, whether private or not, had some effect on those in your world. Our disobedience can even affect those outside our sphere of contact. But there is a second principle that comes from our corporate solidarity, a ripple that is seldom considered but critical to the church's role in this world.

Principle 2: Disobedience Offends God and Destroys the Reputation and Distinctiveness of God's People

> "The Canaanites and the other people of the country will hear about this and they will surround us and wipe out our name from the earth. What then will you do for your own great name?" (Josh. 7:9).

Joshua was a sensitive spiritual leader. Understanding that sin offends the character and honor of the Holy God, he voiced his concern to God that Israel might perish and God's reputation be tarnished. He knew the nation that carried the flag of honor was responsible for upholding that honor.

When a believer is involved in moral compromise, it is an offense against God. David acknowledged this when he repented of his sin with Bathsheba and cried, "Against you [God], you only, have I sinned" (Psa. 51:4). The king's sin was against a woman, her husband, and a nation, but more significantly he understood it first as a breach of his relationship with the living God.

Disappearing Distinctives

One reason Christianity today has been labeled "tasteless" is that the distinctiveness of God's people has

41

been washed out. At times the Christian community is camouflaged. There is so much compromise in the lives of God's people that we're indistinguishable from the world. This brings disdain upon God's reputation and honor. That's exactly what Joshua feared. The glory and honor of God is always trampled under the feet of ungodly people when we give in to wrong.

If this causes you to worry about God, don't. God's glory continues. He is not changed by our mistakes. His honor remains the same. He is constant and consistent. But people's perceptions of God can change. That's where the danger lies. That's what sin does. That's why God was so harsh with Achan. Because of Achan's wrong, the good reputation and distinctiveness of God's people was blurred before the godless nations. Unless the holiness of God is shown to others through the distinctive lifestyle of his people, the world will fail to see its need for forgiveness and reconciliation. They will fail to see their need for a Savior.

Principle 3: Disobedience Weakens the People of God and Makes Them Vulnerable to Enemy Attack

> So about three thousand men went up; but they were routed by the men of Ai, who killed about thirty-six of them. They chased the Israelites from the city gate as far as the stone quarries and struck them down on the slopes. At this the hearts of the people melted and became like water (Joshua 7:4-5).

It's hard to believe that the loss of thirty-six valiant warriors and the resulting fear was caused by one man's sin. Modern man is discovering the hard way that a small act sometimes goes undetected until it destroys many.

Contamination Downstream

Recently the Public Health Department of my hometown received a $100,000 award from Harvard University and the Ford Foundation for developing an ingenious method to detect high levels of pollutants in the city's storm sewers. In the past, a $500 chemical test, administered by men in expensive protective suits, was used to check for contaminants. The new device is so simple, it's embarrassing. The Health Department places a small fish in a perforated plastic jug, weights it down with a brick, and places it into the flowing water of the sewer. If the fish dies (which no one desires), then the inspector knows the level of contamination is too high.

Spiritual pollution operates the same way in the body of Christ. Where there is pollution, deadly effects follow, though we can't see the contaminants until the damage is done. Conversely, it is in purity the fellowship finds its strength.

Wrongs you and I committed last week fracture the body's ability to be wise, to understand, and to live by godly principles. Contamination flows through the Body of Christ and weakens our immune system. Spiritual compromise makes Christians vulnerable and poisons the spiritual bloodstream of the church. But there is a final principle of more concern than the previous three.

Principle 4: Sin Brings the Faded Presence of God

> That is why the Israelites cannot stand against their enemies; they turn their backs and run because they have been made liable to destruction. I will not be with you anymore unless you destroy whatever among you is devoted to destruction (Josh. 7:12).

If there is one thing the Savior's flock needs, it's the caring presence of the Shepherd. But God's holiness and purity are not compatible with the presence of sin. The more we transgress, the less God's divine gifts will be apparent in our lives. God and lawbreaking cannot occupy the same heart space.

Israel had to choose between the Presence of God (v. 12) and the presence of wrong (v. 13). If the Israelites wanted to experience God's smile, they had to choose God over sin.

The key promise made to Joshua was the abiding Presence of his God (1:5,9; 3:7). The main prayer of the people on behalf of Joshua was also for divine Presence (1:17). The basis of Joshua's exaltation (3:7) and the future hope of possessing the land centered around the divine Presence of the Covenant God with his people. But Achan's sin caused that Presence to fade and the nation to experience a loss of direction, power, and spiritual progress. Sin is serious business with God. How can I say it more bluntly?

The Vine and the Branch

God says, "Unless you deal with your sins, I will not be with you anymore." Just as it is essential for a branch to draw its life from the vine, God's presence with us is essential for spiritual power, divine direction, and supernatural vitality. Conversely, rebellion greedily devours our spiritual vitality, both individually and corporately. It causes us to experience that loss of divine presence, the most-needed grace in our lives. God's grace slowly takes a back seat as sin is allowed into the driver's seat.

Yes, we still have salvation and the promises secured by the cross, but daily vitality is lost. The warmth of the divine fire of Christ's Spirit is quenched (1 Thess. 5:19). The pain that sin brings to the heart of God grieves him (Eph. 4:30), and he removes his grace and shepherdly guidance.

Time to Choose

We must wake up to the polluting effect that disobedience is having on the body of Christ. Compromise on the lower floor can climb all the way to the balcony of our sanctuaries. We must choose between sin and the presence of God. We have to love each other and exhort each other to purity and faithfulness. As Francis Schaeffer states with conviction, "The church that seeks God's blessing cannot afford to neglect the purity of the body."[3]

Are you struggling with fear, doubt about your faith, loneliness? All these could be the result of a spiritual void in your life, a void that God's presence should be filling. Do you have anything lurking below the surface? Have you been feeling a loss deep within your spirit, a cavity caused by the fading presence of a grieving Christ? Either we confess our sins before the living God or we send its destructive ripples out to others. It's time to choose to be faithful.

In the pages ahead, I will develop the blueprint that Christ gave the church to keep her pure and healthy. It's a plan the early church practiced and the Reformation rekindled, yet today it's largely ignored.

But before I do, let me assure you, though I may seem pessimistic about the faith, given the signs of the times, I am actually optimistic. I find strength when I remember Paul's words of encouragement:

"No eye has seen
     no ear has heard,

no mind has conceived
  what God has prepared for those who
    love him"

(1 Cor. 2:9).

Paul's words make the struggle worth it all. Christ has waiting for me things I cannot now understand. Even though I may fail or be hurt by others who disappoint, Christ will never fail!

Notes

1. Steven H. Austin, "Mt. St. Helens and Catastrophism," *Impact* 157 (El Cajon, Calif.: Institute for Creation Research, 1986).

2. Marten H. Woudstra, *The Book of Joshua*, New International Commentary on the Old Testament (Grand Rapids, Mich.: Wm. B. Eerdmans Publishing Co., 1981), 120.

3. Francis A. Schaeffer, *Joshua and the Flow of Biblical History* (Downers Grove, Ill.: InterVarsity Press, 1975), 117.

PART Two

The Church on Bedrock

Sealing the Cracks of Time

I had never had an appreciation for the fear that one experiences during an earthquake until one evening as I watched the national news. Two ladies were being interviewed in their front yard. The newsman was probing them about their response to the early morning quake that shook them out of bed when an aftershock hit. Both ladies began to scream and clutch each other, shouting and weeping. Grabbing the side of their trailer home, they begged God, with loud expletives, to cause it to stop.

What happens when you experience a tremor like that? You lose your equilibrium. Your mind alerts your body to the loss of balance and the inevitable consequences of a fall. The prospect of severe injury or even death causes fear and a sinking sense of despair. These ladies gave the nation a lesson on the loss of balance.

Twentieth-century Christianity has experienced a loss of balance. Its sense of stability and integrity has been shaken. There is a crisis of unchecked sin in the church today, and we have lost much of our spiritual equilibrium.

A Search for Stable Ground

Another reason that we have such a tremendous loss of equilibrium today is our neglect of a critical biblical doctrine. It is a doctrine that gives equilibrium, stability, and balance to everything we do in the Kingdom of God, a doctrine that puts the church back on bedrock away from the unstable faultline, a doctrine that comes from the lips of Jesus himself.

Jesus encountered human faults and failures in the midst of his work on earth. The disciples had feet of clay and an inclination to do wrong, just as any disciple today. The Son of God had no misgivings about the problem of sin in the hearts of men. He knew that throughout the centuries the church would suffer from the shakings of sin and the nausea of lost spiritual balance.

To keep his community on solid footing, Jesus gave the disciples a divine blueprint, a game plan intended to keep the church from the trauma she is now suffering. We need to be put back on divine bedrock.

Finding Bedrock

Jesus brought his disciples to Caesarea Philippi, on the northern shore of the Sea of Galilee, for rest and to continue their education. It was there, in this quaint fishing village, that he poured the foundation for the future of the Christian community (Matt. 16:13-19).

The time had come for the Master to give his men the most important quiz in history. The Lord's first question was, "Who do people say the Son of Man is?" Several replies came back. Then, with those piercing eyes, Jesus looked at the men before him and asked, "But what about you? Who do you say I am?"

Simon Peter couldn't hold it in any longer. His hand went up and his mouth flew open, "You are the Christ, the Son of the Living God." Bull's-eye! Peter had "aced" the test.

Responding to Peter, Jesus puts the church on solid bedrock and gives her an eternal blueprint for finding equilibrium even in the toughest times:

> Blessed are you, Simon son of Jonah, for this was not revealed to you by man, but by my Father in heaven. And I tell you that you are Peter, and on this rock I will build my church, and the gates of Hades will not overcome it. I will give you the keys of the kingdom of heaven; whatever you bind on earth will be bound in heaven, and whatever you loose on earth will be loosed in heaven (vv. 17-19).

Within this divine commitment to the apostle, the church today can find the key to its much-needed stability.

The Coming Community

In all his recorded statements, Jesus mentions his church (*ekklesia*) only twice. The first time is in his reply to Peter; the other is found in Matthew 18:17. There is a significant connection between these two usages, but before making the connection, two observations are important.

First, when Jesus spoke these words to Peter, the

church was not yet in existence. Our Lord's statement was a prophetic projection that he knew would soon come to reality. Jesus was looking into the future and instructing these men about the coming spiritual community and the responsibilities that the leadership of the church (men like Peter) would have to embrace. The Scriptures and history record it just as he said. At Pentecost (Acts 2), the bride of Christ was born. The body that every Christian is now a part of came into being.

It was through revelation from God that Peter made his confession (Matt. 16:16), and Jesus affirms that it is upon the foundation of Peter's confession that he will build his church: "And I tell you that you are Peter, and on this rock I will build my church, and the gates of Hades will not overcome it" (v. 18).

Upon the rock of the confession made by Peter and by other followers yet to come, men and women of like faith, Jesus would build his church. Jesus would form the church based on the same faith and confession of thousands of men and women.

Peter does just as Jesus predicted; he restated his confession of faith at Pentecost—"Therefore let all Israel be assured of this: God has made this Jesus, whom you crucified, both Lord and Christ" (Acts 2:36). On that day the church was born, and thousands made a similar confession as Peter concerning the identity of the Messiah. They were people of like faith in the Christ.

Jesus also gives Peter authority to keep the church off the faultline. With confidence, Jesus proclaims to Peter, "I will give you the keys of the kingdom of heaven; whatever you bind on earth will be bound in heaven, and whatever you loose on earth will be loosed in heaven" (Matt. 16:19).

In the promise, two spiritual keys are given: one to lock and the other to unlock. The idea of "loosing and binding" will be addressed later, but Jesus is giving Peter the authority to deal with the problem of sin in the church. Jesus established this authority and responsibility to care for the spiritual purity of his church before she had drawn her first breath.

But how does this authority to discipline have relevance today? Jesus intentionally transferred the authority he gave Peter to all the church, knowing she would need this solid spiritual bedrock in the future.

Two Keys for Stabilizing Today's Church

The second time Jesus refers to the church is in the context of Matthew 18:15-20. This time he is looking down the time tunnel of the ages. From the day of Pentecost to the present, he projects the need to give his corporate body a way to keep pure and holy in the midst of a perverse world:

> If your brother sins against you, go and show him his fault, just between the two of you. If he listens to you, you have won your brother over. But if he will not listen, take one or two others along, so that 'every matter may be established by the testimony of two or three witnesses.' If he refuses to listen to them, tell it to the church; and if he refuses to listen even to the church, treat him as you would a pagan or a tax collector.
>
> I tell you the truth, whatever you bind on earth will be bound in heaven, and whatever you loose on earth will be loosed in heaven.
>
> Again, I tell you that if two of you on earth

agree about anything you ask for, it will be done
for you by my Father in heaven. For where two
or three come together in My name, there am I
with them (Matt. 18:15-20).

Did you notice the critical connection between this
passage and the Matthew 16 passage we looked at earlier?
Both passages talk about "binding and loosing." But in
this case, the authority for binding and loosing belongs to
the church. Christ has moved from addressing Peter to
addressing the Christian community. The authority to deal
with sin and spiritual failure in a loving, restorative fashion
is a responsibility of the church and her leadership (v. 17).

Jesus has, in effect, said to every church leader who
comes after Peter (and to all those who confess Christ as
Savior and Lord), "You have the responsibility and the
authority to deal with sin in the lives of your Christian
brothers and sisters." According to Jesus, should any of us
ever go astray, there must be an all-out effort towards
recovery as soon as possible.[1]

Paul the Practitioner

In the city nestled next to ours, there is a church that
operates a vital ministry. It's reputation is well known.
Over the last years, it has experienced great growth and
spiritual integrity. However, several years ago, the body
took a spiritual torpedo in its side.

The church boasted of a godly leadership, until one
Sunday morning a key elder sat in the front row with a
female companion . . . who was not his wife. The elder's
family sat on the back row. Below the surface, this family
had been experiencing serious relational fractures that
began to bubble to the surface. This open display of

wrong caused the whole fellowship to blush. Even though several whispered behind closed doors, months went by while the elder continued to bring his friend to church, seeking public approval of his new lifestyle.

The family and church were humiliated. The church's testimony was badly damaged as the news was carried outside the fellowship.

What happens to a congregation when they refuse to handle sin in their midst? The apostle Paul believed that spiritual toxins come from unchecked sin—toxins that destabilize the Christian community and cause it to experience a loss of equilibrium. But Paul knew how to handle the problem. He used the keys given by Christ himself.

The apostle wrote almost all we know about the application of the loving discipline set forth by Jesus. The most complete example deals with a case of incest in the local body (1 Cor. 5:1-13), a passage we will examine in more detail in chapter 5. The church's condoning of this sin was a shock even to the pagan community (v.1). Paul understood that a little arrogance about immorality can easily spread like yeast until it pervades the entire church. For the health of the church, Paul instructed them to remove the offender from their midst.

Interpreting Discipline in the New Testament

Additional disciplinary teaching is found in Paul's other epistles, and we will examine those passages in later chapters. But for now, we can make some initial observations about New Testament church discipline as set forth by Jesus and practiced by the early church.

First, there was an insistence on community purity to the extent that even removal of an unrepentant brother was encouraged (1 Cor. 5:9-13; 2 Thess. 3:6-15). Sin posed a grave threat to the local church.

Second, there was a heavy emphasis on building a community whose lifestyle was distinctive from the world around it (1 Cor. 6:2, 9-11).

Third, discipline was a tool used by the church to preserve holiness, avoid contamination, and stimulate spiritual growth (2 Cor. 7:11; Gal. 6:1-2).

Finally, discipline was an act of love used to bring repentance and restoration in the life of the errant brother or sister. With discipline comes hope for renewal (1 Cor. 5:6-8).

The Great Reformation

Corrective discipline was prominent in the post-apostolic church. Unfortunately, syncretism with the Roman world caused the practice to lapse. When pagan rituals began to be welcomed into the early church, biblical practices fell aside.

During the Middle Ages, discipline was distorted and abused. A gradual shift to private penance and a new custom of confession to the priest led to a highly impersonal and mechanical form of discipline that was foreign to the New Testament. Personal repentance and reconciliation were replaced by penance through duties and regulations. Some historians believe the Reformation was sparked by a reaction against this system of penance. Not until the sixteenth century do we see a significant return of New Testament discipline to the daily life of the church.

With the Reformation, a fresh breeze of change blew across the church. A return to biblical principles sparked a return to properly exercised discipline. Parts of the Reformation movement embraced Jesus' teachings as a divine set of blueprints given to help his church. One example is the Belgic Confession (1561), which considers church discipline one of the three marks of the true church:

> The marks by which the true church is known are these: If the pure doctrine of the gospel is preached therein, if she maintains the pure administration of the sacraments as instituted by Christ, if church discipline is exercised in punishing sin; in short, if all things are managed according to the pure Word of God, all things contrary thereto rejected, and Jesus Christ acknowledged as the only Head of the Church. (The Belgic Confession XXIX)

Two other major confessions echo the same truth. The Heidelberg Catechism views discipline as one of the two keys of the Kingdom of Heaven (Questions 83 and 85). The Westminster Confession devotes a detailed article to discipline (Article 30), describing its power, purpose, and procedure.

Within the Reformation period, the Anabaptists were the most outspoken and committed to the practice. They attempted to follow the New Testament by purifying their fellowships through loving confrontation of error. They were the first to label this practice "the rule of Christ," because it was given by the Lord as an eternal rule for maintaining purity in the church. They believed each church was responsible to exercise discipline, and they held the motto, "No discipline, no church."

Throughout the Reformation, the church issued fresh statements of the need for discipline and the spiritual vigor that it would bring to the body of Christ. John Smyth, founder of the first English Baptist congregation in Holland, was so impressed with the transformation of the members of his congregation due to corrective discipline that he could write a friend:

> Oh, Mr. Bernard, if you knew but the comfort and power of the Lord's ordinances of admonition and excommunication as we do (blessed be our good God) in some measure, and that growth and reformation which is in some of us thereby, you would be so wonderfully ravished with the power of God's ordinances that you would acknowledge the Church to be terrible as an army with banners, and yet enjoyable and lovely, comely and beautiful.[2]

A Healthy History

Some Wesleyan scholars believe that the implementation of this doctrine was the number one reason Methodism was the fastest growing and eventually the largest denomination in the history of Christendom. When the movement came to the American colonies, it spread across the entire continent in less than a hundred years, absorbing as many people for the cause of Christ as any other movement in history.

History verifies that when exercised according to the Lord's prescription, discipline acts as a purifying and cleansing agent that brings spiritual vitality to the church and her people.

Where Has All the Discipline Gone?

The religious community committed to moral values and biblical holiness has been forced to deal with discipline from the beginning. As Jesus instituted it and Paul practiced it, corrective discipline brings to the Kingdom of Christ purity, intimacy with God, and distinctiveness in the world. Since the church has lost much of its influence, there is a pressing need to reassess the doctrine from both biblical and historical perspectives.

Jesus himself has given us a timeless blueprint for dealing with sin in the body. There should be no indifference to wrongdoing. Since corrective discipline is so valuable, why are most Christians unwilling to use it? The next chapter reveals seven reasons Christians today don't dare to discipline.

Notes

1. Harold O. J. Brown, "The Role of Discipline in the Church," *Covenant Quarterly (CovQ)*, August 1983, 51.

2. John Smyth, "Parallels, Consensus, and Observations," *The Works of John Smyth*, ed. W. T. Whiting (Cambridge: Cambridge University Press, 1915), 441.

CHAPTER FOUR

Seven Reasons Why Christians Don't Dare to Discipline

How easy it is to misunderstand biblical truth, especially when the truth is personally threatening.

In our church, we greet visitors and interested church shoppers with a warm and open opportunity we call the "Pastor's Welcome Class." I'm usually at the helm every Sunday, being lighthearted, sharing a cup of coffee, and interacting with the visitors. Each week I try to communicate a distinctive about our fellowship to acquaint the newcomer with our philosophy of ministry. It's always fun, informative, and low pressure, but on one occasion it backfired.

I flipped on the overhead and turned my notes to the subject of New Testament discipline. Our church embraces this doctrine as a responsibility of every church. I presented a simple overview; the teaching seemed to be well received. But one couple, Daryl and Linda, walked out the door and never came back.

A Tragic Misunderstanding

Over the next few weeks, I looked for Daryl and Linda. They were good friends of one of our pillar families. I wanted them to be comfortable, and I hoped they would get involved. Where were they? With concern, I decided to find out.

When Daryl answered the telephone, his voice betrayed an uncomfortable edginess. He was polite but unresponsive. I decided to quickly cut through the fog: "Have we offended you? What happened to push you away from us?" There was silence. When he finally spoke, his words were sharp: "Frankly, Linda and I were frightened by your church's view on discipline."

I probed for a minute to find the source of the fear. Was it my teaching? Was it my demeanor? Did my overhead transparencies need more color? Unamused, he responded, "No, we were just afraid that some Saturday afternoon you might drop by our home and find me working in the yard, shirtless, and drinking a cold beer." That was it! What a misunderstanding.

In the mind of many Christians, the same misunderstanding exists. Words such as *trial, punitive, accused,* and *guilty* seem to follow the teaching. And yet, the Lord never used such language.

So what is corrective discipline, and what is it not? Why should it be practiced? Correctly defining the doctrine would resolve many of our misperceptions.

Understanding the Gift of Discipline

Before examining the purpose for discipline, let's define it. Corrective church discipline is *the process by which a local church works to restore a professing Christian who has fallen into sin.* The sinning Christian may be a leader of a whole denomination or a low-profile member of a small rural church. The process applies in both cases.

What It Is Not

Church discipline is not legalism—a preoccupation with externals and the letter of the law. Such misapplication of biblical principles has always been a part of the doctrine and has brought great tragedy to people's lives. The church does not need any more legalism or rigid codes of conduct to keep her away from the real job of loving one another. Christians could easily turn this needed teaching against others and inflict abuse.

Church discipline is not court trials or codes of punishment. It is not a "smut search" giving every believer license to shove a magnifying glass over the activities of other brothers and sisters. It should not be viewed as punishment nor as a tool to protect a congregation's reputation. According to the language used by Christ and the methods used by Paul, church discipline has a much higher purpose.

What It Is

Jesus gives the main purpose for exercising discipline in Matthew 18:15, "If your brother sins against you, go and show him his fault, just between the two of you. If he listens to you, you have won your brother over."

The purpose for discipline is to bring a Christian to spiritual restoration and reconciliation. If the sinning brother repents, he is reconciled to God and to the church. When we've accomplished that, we've "won our brother over." It is an obligation and also a privilege to convey to an erring fellow believer the truth that Jesus loves him and that reconciliation with God and the Christian community is necessary and possible. Paul adds:

> Brothers, if someone is caught in a sin, you who are spiritual should restore him gently. But watch yourself, or you also may be tempted. Carry each other's burdens, and in this way you will fulfill the law of Christ (Gal. 6:1-2).

Paul's exhortation sets the exercise of discipline in the context of love and gentleness. Did you notice the words:

> brother . . .
>   restore . . .
>   gently . . .
>   carry?

We are not to think of the person as accused or on trial but in need of restoration and forgiveness through tender, properly motivated love. Even when Paul encouraged the ultimate discipline—excommunication—reconciliation of the erring brother was still the goal (1 Cor. 5:1-10). Author Ron Sider sees this emphasis when he writes:

> If the goal of church discipline is restoration and reconciliation, then the attitudes and language we use should reflect that goal. Language about "the accused," "court," "trial," or "punishment" has no place whatsoever in church discipline. If Jesus calls the person who is sinning a brother, then we dare not think of him as the accused.[1]

The context of the key biblical teaching by Jesus provides additional support for restoration and reconciliation being the purpose of discipline. In Matthew 18:6-9, Jesus issues a warning not to cause others to sin. Then in verses 12-14, he tells the parable of the lost sheep with its theme of God's love for every sheep in his fold. Those who go astray are still loved and sought out. Many times, brothers and sisters in Christ are responsible for that search-and-find mission. The scriptures on discipline instruct Christians to search out those who have gone astray. We should love them back into the fold just as Christ would.

Immediately after Christ's teaching on discipline, Matthew records Peter's well-known question, "How many times shall I forgive my brother when he sins against me?" How many times must we forgive the person who has hurt and disappointed us? The Lord's answer—"seventy times seven"—indicates we are to forgive an unlimited number of times. We are to forgive because we are called to love them as the Good Shepherd loves them.

The desire to restore and reconcile the offender to ourselves and to God is foremost. If God forgives the repentant sinner seventy times seven, solely through Christ's saving merit, then the thought of punishment should never cross our minds. Restoration and forgiveness are at the heart of the biblical blueprint for church discipline. Healing is the goal.

You might say we are called to "watch over one another in love."[2] Since Christians exist as a distinctive body, if one member suffers from moral failure, we all suffer. Therefore, loving discipline is for the benefit of all. That's why we should consider the responsibility of discipline as a gift.

The gifts which Jesus gives are designed to build

up our one body. As each person exercises his or
her gift, other brothers and sisters overcome
their selfish, sinful desires and grow toward that
mature personhood which our Lord Jesus lived
to perfection (Eph. 4:11-13). We can help each
other grow toward that mature personhood by
watching over each other in love, gently, restoring those who stray.[3]

At its foundation, discipline is actually an exercise of
evangelism. Both demand that the gospel be declared.

Church discipline is a loving proclamation of the
good news that God always accepts and trans-
forms the sinner who repents. Biblical repentance, of course, is not just a brief ritual in
which one sheds a tear and repeats a formula
about justification alone. Biblical repentance
involves conversion: a turning around, a turning
away from former sins.[4]

Just as repentance and claiming the forgiveness that
Christ purchased on the cross is the only condition for
entering into the body of Christians, so in discipline,
repentance is the condition for continued relationship with
both Christ and the church.

Corrective discipline, then, deals with repentance, with
restoration, with watching over one another in love. It has
to do with caring, with spiritual stability, with loving each
other. If the church would exercise this doctrine properly, it
would remove most of the scandals and shams destroying
people's lives. If someone would say to the one on the edge
of the faultline, "Wait a minute. Is what you're doing
right?" we would be watching over one another in love and
doing much to prevent major aftershocks.

If the young couple who visited my class had not misunderstood, they might still be involved in Christian growth. How important it is to understand the purpose and goals of church discipline. Tragically, not only do Christians misunderstand, but entire denominations and society as a whole ignore the practice.

The primary reason for the absence of loving discipline today is a lack of biblical understanding of its *purpose*. Add to this the six reasons summarized below, and it is easy to see why loving discipline is neglected by the church.

1. The Prevalence of the "Every-Man-Is-an-Island" Attitude

Believers in Christ have bought into the laissez-faire spirit of our age. Too many Christians have become brash, individualistic, isolated people. They don't understand the need for community, the biblical truth that the group is more important than just *me*. Their attitude is, "Do your own thing and don't come near me; don't snoop into my life; stay away." As a result, they draw away from community accountability.

This relativistic, "do your own thing" morality has made an indelible impact on our ability to make moral judgments. Some of the sins that automatically led to ecclesiastical censure and possible excommunication in the past (i.e., homosexuality) are now regarded by the church as justifiable or, at the very least, understandable.

Interestingly, in the midst of the great need for spiritual stability, there are those critics who insist that the church remain nonintrusive and nonjudgmental.[5] The church should offer solace and acceptance and stay out of a Christian's private world. They maintain that passing moral judgment is outside the church's arena of competence.

However, those who see church discipline as "spiritual judgmentalism" are in part responsible for fostering the idea that discipline is an invasion of the sanctity of the soul rather than a spiritual salve for restoration and healing.

The move away from community accountability and toward religious individualism is a distressing development that destroys efforts to exercise discipline.

The emphasis on personal experience would eventually override all efforts at church discipline. Already in the eighteenth century, it was possible for individuals to find the form of religion that best suited their inclinations. By the nineteenth century, religious bodies had to compete in a consumer's market and grew or declined in terms of changing patterns of individual religious taste.[6]

The church needs to maintain its position and refuse to become a compromised religious group whose thoughts are shaped by culture rather than by biblical perspectives.

2. A Disrespect for Authority within the Church

The anti-institution mood of the last twenty-five years has effectively eroded the authority of the church. In contrast to previous generations in which disciplinary actions by the church created spiritual trepidation, such measures have become, in some circles, a comical matter. What purpose does it serve to mete out discipline when there is respect neither for the office bearer of the church nor for the church itself?

Ironically, the absence of discipline has taken from the church a platform on which authority could be displayed. The church seldom exerts authority in any area of religious life; therefore, authority is not respected. Historian Winthrop Hudson states as much in a revealing survey of how the self-worth of American churches has declined.

> So casual were the demands of the churches, even in terms of such responsibilities as attendance and payment of dues, that the pull of emotional loyalty to a college fraternity, social club, lodge, trade union, professional association or veterans association frequently exceeds that exerted by the church.[7]

3. Differing Denominational Policies

Some denominations have, in essence, no discipline. Others are lax in the application of whatever rules they may still embrace. Consequently, anyone who is censured in one church can leave it and, without difficulty, join another. This substantially reduces the effectiveness of the disciplinary action or censure.

4. Confusion Concerning Christian Accountability and the Local Church

There is much confusion about the job description of the local church. Few Christians today desire to be held accountable by other believers. Yet to belong to the Lord is to belong to his church (1 Cor. 12:13) and to submit to the discipline of his people (Matt. 18:15-18; Gal. 6:1-2). Many Christians have a poor understanding of the local church and its authority. They do not see the importance of spiritual accountability.

Ben Patterson warns us about the delusions of private religion when he says that "the man who seeks God in isolation from his fellows is likely to find, not God, but the

Devil, who will bear an embarrassing resemblance to himself."[8]

While the church has been guilty of flagrant abuses when exercising discipline in the past, this is no reason to exclude the proper exercise of loving discipline today. We don't give up on marriage just because so many make a mess of it. We cannot abandon the clear biblical call for church discipline just because others have handled it poorly.

5. The Pragmatic Problem of Revenue Loss

Discipline is often short-circuited by the fear of an empty offering plate. Tragically, the church leadership may fear starting a cleansing action that might bring dissatisfaction and revolt. Private probing can quickly clamp shut the pocketbook of parishioners.

This is nothing short of a compromise with truth. I believe Jesus would have a strong statement to make about such an attitude. The local church cannot be true to her Lord without practicing discipline whenever the need arises . . . regardless of the cost. The Scriptures command us to do so.

6. Rising Fear of the Law

Another deterrent to the exercise of discipline is the possibility that those who practice it might end up in court! More and more churches fear legal backlash if they make any attempt to exercise discipline in a parishioner's life.

The Church of Christ in Collinsville, Oklahoma, received a $1.35 million lawsuit filed by a disciplined member. This thirty-six-year-old single woman charged the church and its elders with "invasion of privacy and willful intent to inflict emotional distress." After a four-day trial, the Tulsa jury ruled in her favor and awarded $390,000. Even though some feel the discipline and public disclosure were mishandled, and that the church elders "overextended the bounds of their responsibility when they reported their actions to four neighboring congregations,"[9] the outcome has awakened the legal community to a new arena of possible litigation.[10]

However, the biblical mandate must be obeyed with love and sensitivity, and the process must be handled properly or the church will continue to suffer from *more* than legal action. Charles Colson, founder and president of Prison Fellowship, responding to the Collinsville case writes,

> It will be sad news if the court should emasculate the church by holding that it can't enforce biblical standards on its members; but it will be even worse news if it turns out that by ignoring our biblical responsibilities we have done it to ourselves.[11]

Rippling through Our Homes

The absence of discipline has done more than emasculate and weaken our churches. It has also wreaked havoc on our Christian homes.

> As I think of the homes that have been hopelessly broken, the estrangements that have permanently resulted, and the misery that has been unnecessarily caused by the failure of churches to practice church discipline, or to practice it biblically, my heart aches. Even more tragically, as I consider the ruins of many congregations torn by schismatic and factious toxin of

71

unrepentant sin that circulates in Christ's body of believers, I am deeply moved.[12]

A Strangling Bride

The contemporary bride is being strangled by confusion and fear. Daniel Wray writes, "The modern church seems more willing to ignore sin than to denounce it, and more ready to compromise God's Law than to proclaim it."[13] Emil Bruner recognizes the relationship between the lack of discipline and some of the paralysis of the church when he says, "the lack of exercised discipline is a sign of miserable weakness."[14] Bruner's statement is a telling commentary.

Christ's loving care over the church is evidenced in his disciplinary action. Revelation 3:19 portrays him as the righteous judge in the midst of his people, dealing actively with their sin. Likewise the church, his Bride, has the responsibility to deal with unrepentant sin in its midst.

In the next chapter, I'll show how even the smallest practice of discipline benefits you and every member of the local body. When we do things heaven's way, everyone on earth receives a benefit.

Notes

1. Ron Sider, "Watching Over One Another . . . in Love," *The Other Side Magazine*, May-June 1975, 18.

2. Ibid., 13.

3. Ibid., 15.

4. Ibid.

5. Alvin L. Hoksbergen, "Excommunication, A 'No' Vote," *The Banner*, August 1981, 12. Hoksbergen holds that the practice of church discipline has driven many from the church, causing deep hurt and bitterness.

6. Robert N. Bellah, *Habits of the Heart: Individualism and Commitment in American Life* (New York: Harper & Row, 1985), 233.

7. Winthrop Hudson, *The Great Tradition of the American Churches* (Grand Rapids, Mich.: Wm. B. Eerdman's Publishing Co., 1980), 247-48.

8. Ben Patterson, "Discipline: The Backbone of the Church," *Leadership*, 4 (Winter 1983):111.

9. Carl Laney, *A Guide to Church Discipline* (Minneapolis: Bethany House Publishers, 1985), 134

10. A brief, but thorough, summary of the legal history of church discipline litigation is provided by Ronald B. Flowers, "Can Churches Discipline Members and Win in Court?" *Journal of Church and State* 27 (Autumn 1985):483-98. Another detailed and well-organized work on the problems and solutions of court litigation can be found in Lynn Buzzard and Thomas S. Brandon's *Church Discipline and the Courts* (Wheaton, Ill.: Tyndale House, 1987).

11. Chuck Colson, "The Church Should Mind Its Own Business," *Jubilee*, April 1984, 3.

12. Jay Adams, *Handbook of Church Discipline* (Grand Rapids, Mich.: Zondervan Publishing House, 1986), 8.

13. Daniel Wray, *Biblical Church Discipline* (Carlisle, Penn.: The Banner of Truth and Trust, 1978), 1.

14. Emil Bruner, *The Divine Imperative* (Philadelphia: Westminster Press, 1947), 559.

CHAPTER FIVE

Something for Everyone:
Heaven's Answer to Earth's Faultline

The drawbacks and abuses that flow from corrective discipline cause some Christians to ask, Why do it? Doesn't it do more harm than good? Why not allow the problems in our fellowship and in our personal lives to continue unaddressed? After all, Christianity seems to march forward without it.

Such attitudes ignore the hurt and embarrassment that unchecked sin brings both to the body of Christ and to the individual involved in the error. Our need for purity and the holiness of God demands that discipline be practiced.

The abuses that can accompany improperly applied discipline stem from losing sight of some key questions. What outcome does God desire for the body of Christ?

What are the objectives of properly exercised discipline? Why should the church discipline a wayward member, and what is the benefit to the one being disciplined?

The New Testament establishes more than the traditional dual purposes of *reformation of the offender* and *preservation of the purity of the church*. Rather, the Scriptures reveal a wide variety of purposes. Specifically, I find four categories of Christians who benefit from the loving exercise of discipline: *the offender*, the entire *local church*, the *individual believer in the body*, and the *leadership* of the church.

You might want to take a pencil and get ready to do some underlining in this chapter. Corrective discipline is heaven's answer to the sin problem in all our lives.

The Purposes of Discipline in the Life of the Offender

An examination of three key passages will show the value and objectives for disciplinary action in the offender's life.

Purpose 1: To restore and reconcile the offender to God and to the fellowship.

Caught in Sin (Galatians 6:1)

Galatians 5 teaches that "the deeds of the flesh" (5:19-21) are not to characterize any Christian. Rather, the fruits of God's Holy Spirit should always be visible on the surface of a committed life (5:22-23). However, the apostle Paul is realistic. He knows that sin will occur in the Christian community, and when it does, it must be addressed:

> Brothers, if someone is caught in a sin, you who
> are spiritual should restore him gently. But

76

watch yourself, or you also may be tempted.

The first value of discipline for the life of a Christian floundering in sin is to restore and reconcile him to God and to the church. The Greek word for *restore* is used in the Gospels to refer to the mending of torn or tangled fishing nets. Discipline takes a life torn and tangled and restores it to usability.

Sin Detectives. Does Paul's use of the phrase "caught in a sin" imply that the offender must first be "caught in the act" before he is confronted? I don't believe Paul has this narrow meaning in mind. A better understanding is that the brother is caught "by sin" or "ensnared by the deceitfulness of sin."[1]

Restoration should be attempted when a person in the congregation has committed a sin that has come to the attention of other believers. Paul is not suggesting that believers should go around "snooping" in the private lives of others.

Spiritually Qualified. Did you notice to whom Paul assigned this responsibility of approaching the errant brother? "You who are spiritual." Reflecting back on Galatians 5, it's easy to see what Paul is thinking. He has in view those who are under the Spirit's control and characterized by the fruit of the Spirit (Gal. 5:16, 22-24). Spiritual maturity is a qualification for dealing with sin in the lives of others. Those who are weak and easily tempted (Gal. 6:1) or who are unable to forgive, should allow others to take the lead in the task of discipline.

The elders and deacons of the church should be at the top of the list of those "who are spiritual." Both 1 Timothy 3:1-13 and Titus 1:5-9 put forth the highest standards of spirituality for anyone serving in those leadership capacities. Those qualified by biblical standards are responsible to approach the errant brother. However, a healthy congregation should have many who could tackle the task.

A Special Attitude. The proper attitude for the one approaching the offender is a "spirit of gentleness." Those involved in restoring erring saints are to cultivate meekness, remembering that they, too, may be tempted. Our own vulnerability to temptation should prevent self-righteousness in the treatment of those who have fallen.

Galatians 6:1 establishes that the chief purpose for any discipline is the restoration of the offender, regardless of the magnitude of the sin. The spiritual need of the erring sheep is the focus.

Purpose 2: To shame the offender leading to restoration to the fellowship and a godly lifestyle.

Busy Bodies but Not Busy (2 Thessalonians 3:14-15)

If anyone does not obey our instruction in this letter, take special note of him. Do not associate with him, in order that he may feel ashamed. Yet do not regard him as an enemy, but warn him as a brother.

The Thessalonians were a sensitive and obedient group (1 Thess. 1:6-7). However, a few in the church couldn't seem to maintain their balance. They adopted the "Jesus is returning any day" mentality and conveniently stopped their daily work. (I confess there are days I'd like to do the same thing!) Abusing Christian charity by laziness and refusing to be self-supporting is seen as a sin in God's Word. To make matters worse, it is probable that these spiritual vagrants went from house to house, living off others and spreading gossip (2 Thess. 3:6-12).

While some members dished out food, the busybodies

dished out gossip and slander. This was an intolerable burden for the church. If the attitude became widespread, it would tarnish the good example of Christian faith which the church had won for itself. So Paul writes sternly:

> If anyone does not obey our instruction in this letter, take special note of him. Do not associate with him, in order that he may feel ashamed. Yet do not regard him as an enemy, but warn him as a brother.

Heaven's purpose, then, in the life of an idle gossip is to shame him into self-evaluation and a return to his proper role in the community.

While I have never struggled with "lazy" Christians in my church, gossip seems to find its way into every congregation. The seriousness of the offense then and now is that unruly brothers threaten the peace of the church. Therefore, the discipline Paul advises is not designed just to humiliate the fallen saint, but to force him to a self-examination of his action.

Handle with Care. In verses 14-15, the church is instructed to observe two practical steps. The first step is "to take note," to identify the offender (v. 14). The offending Christian as well as the church should be notified. Second, the church is to practice a qualified separation: "do not associate with him" (v. 15). The proper motive for this action is "that he may feel ashamed," or be stimulated to take spiritual inventory leading to repentance.

A Special Attitude. Paul is quick to add that the attitude of those exercising discipline is also important: "do not regard him as an enemy." Be sensitive. The offender is still "a brother," and there must be no motive to hurt.

The goal is to restore the offender, not ostracize him.

Purpose 3: To destroy fleshly lusts and return the believer to the rule of Christ.

Puffed-Up and Proud of It (1 Corinthians 5:1-5)

> It is actually reported that there is sexual immorality among you, and of a kind that does not occur even among pagans: A man has his father's wife. And you are proud! Shouldn't you rather have been filled with grief and have put out of your fellowship the man who did this? Even though I am not physically present, I am with you in spirit. And I have already passed judgment on the one who did this, just as if I were present. When you are assembled in the name of our Lord Jesus and I am with you in spirit, and the power of our Lord Jesus is present, hand this man over to Satan, so that the sinful nature may be destroyed and his spirit saved on the day of the Lord.

Paul heard that a case of vile sexual sin existed in the church at Corinth. The report had come to him that "a man has his father's wife." It is not clear if the couple were married, but it appears there is a continuing relationship without repentance. The situation was so bad that even the local non-Christians were repulsed. Of course, intercourse with one's mother or stepmother was strictly forbidden in the law (Lev. 18:7-8; 20:11; Deut. 22:30; 27:20), and the historian Josephus labeled this type of offense "as one of the greatest crimes."[2]

To Paul's surprise, the Corinthians were proud of what this man was doing. They actually applauded it. Perhaps the church had adopted a view of freedom that exempted them from the law and its restraints.

> Paul preached freedom from the law in Corinth
> when he founded the community. Some of the
> members understood him to mean that a law
> like Lev. 18:8 was therefore no longer binding.[3]

The church had concluded that because they were
new in Christ, sin was irrelevant to them; their salvation
was complete. Paul says that had the church displayed
godly sorrow, they would have removed the offender from
their midst. Instead, they were puffed up with spiritual
pride.

The practice of removal from the fellowship was
apparently already known to the church since Paul is surprised that the offender has not yet been expelled. Now it
becomes necessary for the apostle to intervene, and he
may be forced to come to them with a whip because of
their complacency (4:21).

The next two verses (5:4-5) are a general statement
to the church with a specific purpose in view for the
offender:

> When you are assembled in the name of our
> Lord Jesus and I am with you in spirit, and the
> power of our Lord Jesus is present, hand this
> man over to Satan, so that the sinful nature may
> be destroyed and his spirit saved on the day of
> the Lord.

Into Satan's Hands? Verse 5 contains many difficul-
ties. That "delivering someone over to Satan" is describing
formal removal from fellowship is not doubted, but it is
hard to determine what precisely was involved or what was
Paul's desired outcome. Apparently the act had a two-fold
objective: the destruction of the flesh and the saving of the

spirit. But how did this play out in the errant brother's life?

To expel this fallen brother is to remove him from the Lord's protective spiritual umbrella, which all servants enjoy, and to make him vulnerable to the destructive influences of Satan. Paul is banishing him from the church to the realm where Satan reigns. This conclusion is strengthened by the answer to another question the passage raises.

The Destruction of the Flesh. What does the apostle mean by "the destruction of the flesh?" If he doesn't mean physical death, then what?

In the New Testament, *the flesh* often represents human self-sufficiency in opposition to dependency on God. It can indicate human acts of self-centeredness apart from Christ. The flesh represents the independent will of man standing in rebellion against God. It's the "I'll do it my way" spirit. Unchecked indulgence can bring a Christian to destruction and act as a wake-up call to his spiritual life. Proverbs 29:6 tells us that "an evil man is snared by his own sin."

> The flesh, the seat of evil passions, had been triumphing over the spirit or new principle implanted in the man's heart by the gospel. The last possible means for undoing this work was excommunication. Thus, by delivering the man over to Satan, the triumphant flesh could develop unchecked. By their very excess and extremes the lusts of the flesh would defeat themselves. The discipline would then have been effective. Whether or not there was a further implication, *the words of Paul meant excommunication from the fellowship in the church.* This discipline was to be exercised by

the assembled church and for a definite purpose.[4]

Indirectly, Satan would become God's tool for restoration. "The ultimate objective was that the 'spirit,' the spiritual life, crushed by the 'flesh,' might be rekindled and saved in the great day on which the Lord will appear as Judge."[5] Paul's hope is that someday, at the end of a scarred and broken life of self-indulgence, the brother will respond to the discipline and return to the Savior.

Removal from Fellowship. To summarize, Paul is excommunicating the errant, unrepentant brother, thrusting him out of the realm of Christ into the realm of Satan so that his self-reliant lifestyle might be destroyed (as repentance would demonstrate), and he might return to reliance on God. This is tough love, but if it works, the result would be worth it. A fallen brother would have returned to the Lordship of Christ.

But what impact does discipline have on the entire church fellowship that observes it? Do even the uninvolved members receive spiritual benefit?

The Purposes of Discipline in the Life of the Local Church

Disciplinary action also has a valuable effect upon the local church. The impact of sin on a local fellowship is debilitating. As Achan's sin prevented Israel from victory against her enemies (Joshua 7:13), so sin in the church gives the enemies of God occasion to blaspheme (Romans 2:24; cf. 1 Timothy 6:1). Removal of sin restores the honor of God, enabling the testimony of the church to shine brightly in the world. When a church has lost its discipline, it has lost its soul. That's why the church must discipline or die.[6]

Purpose 1: To purify the worship and message of the church.

Keep a Clean Batch (1 Corinthians 5:6-8)

In 1 Corinthians 5:6-8, Paul turns his attention from the incestuous offender back to the congregation, criticizing them for their pride and their failure to confront this open sin in their congregation: "Your boasting is not good. Don't you know that a little yeast works through the whole batch of dough?" (v. 6). Out of the metaphor of yeast rises a key purpose of discipline for the local church. One corrupt member is sufficient to corrupt a whole church. Because sin can and does spread, boasting should cease and discipline should begin.

Paul is less concerned about the evil example of the incestuous brother than he is that *tolerance* of his conduct implies acceptance. The purity of the fellowship is the purpose for discipline in Paul's mind. Sin is to be removed from the corporate life so that the fellowship can be as pure practically as it is positionally.

In verse 7, Paul gives the reason why the corporate body should stay pure: "For Christ, our Passover lamb, has been sacrificed." The image is of the Passover feast in Exodus 12 with its unleavened bread and paschal lamb. Even as the Passover carried with it an imperative of purity for Israel, so the crucifixion of Christ demands purity in the church. Paul is calling the church back to a purification of lifestyle by removing sin from the congregation, sin that Jesus died to remove.

Let's face the truth. The world considers the church hypocritical when sin is not dealt with in the congregation.

The one thing the world expects the church to do is say no to sin! Purity is essential for the worship and witness of the church.

> It must be remembered that the church is not some kind of "mutual insurance company" whose object is to protect its individual members in every situation. Rather, it is a fellowship with a purpose of representing Christ to the world, and demonstrating truth and righteousness. Christ commits His honor to the church's keeping. Therefore, the purity of its testimony must be maintained at all costs.[7]

Imagine the purity that would be displayed in the local church if every Christian accepted the responsibility to go to other Christians involved in some offense with the desire to lovingly and gently bring them to repentance.

Discipline and the purity that results from it are essential to the evangelistic outreach of the local body. When sin is addressed, the message of the gospel takes on a supernatural power to reach others.

Purpose 2: To deny the enemy any advantage or access into the church.

Keep the Front Door Closed to Satan (2 Corinthians 2:5-11)

Second Corinthians 2:5-11 deals with a Christian who, after being disciplined, repented of the offense. Yes, it does happen; there are success stories. Paul now encourages the church to relax its discipline because the one excommunicated has repented and desires to return to fellowship:

> The punishment inflicted on him by the majority

is sufficient for him. Now instead, you ought to forgive and comfort him, so that he will not be overwhelmed by excessive sorrow. I urge you, therefore, to reaffirm your love for him. . . . If you forgive anyone, I also forgive him. And what I have forgiven—if there was anything to forgive—I have forgiven in the sight of Christ for your sake, in order that Satan might not outwit us. For we are not unaware of his schemes.

Here lies the heart of Paul's purpose. To leave the repentant brother in Satan's realm would let the devil exceed the limits of his authority and allow him to destroy both the repentant sinner and the congregation (2:11). Paul is reminding the Corinthians of the dangers that the "schemes of Satan" can bring to the church.

Satan might have tried to cause the Christians to become "excessively harsh and rigorous" or he may have tried to cause dissension among them. Again, he may have intended to turn Paul against them because of their sin, and the Corinthian church against Paul because of his strict demands in this issue. In any case, Paul wanted the breach in the church to be healed as quickly as possible so that Satan might not turn this situation into a victory for himself.[8]

A Subtle Danger in the Local Church. The enemy is clever and can work shrewd destruction in the area of church discipline. If the church *does not* practice discipline, Satan has the church defeated in power and effectiveness. If the church *does* practice discipline, he tries to drive the church to extremes in its exercise. Impressing the church to refuse a repentant brother or sister is one of his schemes. The local church needs to practice discipline, even the expulsion of a member when necessary, but it must do so with wisdom, with gentleness, and with a readiness to forgive and to restore quickly.

Purpose 3: To avoid giving God cause to set himself against the local church.

Spiritual Jeopardy (Revelation 2:5)

When you read chapters 2 and 3 of Revelation, one spiritual principle is inescapable: Undisciplined sin can bring divine displeasure and judgment. Note the warning Christ gives to a church that has undisciplined sin in its midst:

> Remember the height from which you have fallen!
> Repent and do the things you did at first. If you
> do not repent, I will come to you and remove
> your lampstand from its place (2:5).

In this context, the lampstand refers to the church's outreach and testimony. If the church fails to respond to the sin in her pews, then its light will be dimmed. Divine judgment will eventually visit like a bolt of lightning, a tragedy every Christian should fear.

The Purposes of Discipline in the Life of the Individual Church Member

Three passages in the New Testament (1 Tim. 1:18-20; 2 Cor. 7:11; Heb. 3:13) clearly show the benefit that disciplining an offender has on other members of the body.

Purpose 1: To assist in strengthening one's faith and maintenance of a clear conscience.

Education through Punishment (1 Timothy 1:18-20)

Timothy, my son, I give you this instruction in

keeping with the prophecies once made about you, so that by following them you may fight the good fight, holding on to faith and a good conscience. Some have rejected these and so have shipwrecked their faith. Among them are Hymenaeus and Alexander, whom I have handed over to Satan to be taught not to blaspheme.

Paul's first letter to Timothy, the young pastor, contains practical insights concerning the exercise of discipline. The apostle describes the action he took against two men who had jettisoned the faith—Hymenaeus and Alexander (1:19-20). These men had consciously yielded to sin and turned their backs on Christ. For such actions, the apostle found it necessary to deliver them over to Satan that they might be brought to their spiritual senses (v. 20). However, Paul's focus is not on the two apostates but on what Timothy is to learn by observing their punishment. Paul wants the young preacher, and every Christian, to learn from observing the lives of those who have sinned and been removed.

The Christian who believes that discipline against sin is necessary and who sees it exercised in a local body will be motivated to keep a clear conscience. The discipline these brothers experienced serves as a warning for Timothy and every member of his local fellowship.

Purpose 2: To promote intense self-examination in each church member's life.

A Personal Sin Check (2 Corinthians 7:11)

Previously, the apostle slapped the church's hand for her unwillingness to deal with sin and obey his apostolic instruction. Now the situation has flipped. Paul has learned of the church's complete obedience; the conflict is over and the breach healed. So he writes:

See what this godly sorrow has produced in you:
what earnestness, what eagerness to clear yourselves, what indignation, what alarm, what long-
ing, what concern, what readiness to see justice
done. At every point you have proved yourselves
to be innocent in this matter.

The Corinthians were called to an intense self-
examination, one that yielded positive spiritual results.
The discipline of the brother brought a godly sorrow for
sin to the whole church and, with it, a desire to put their
house in order. One member committed an offense, and
the whole church is called to self-appraisal and repentance.

Purpose 3: To confirm each believer's responsibility
for members of the body.

Keeping Soft to Sin (Hebrews 3:13)

But encourage one another daily, as long as it is
called Today, so that none of you may be hardened by sin's deceitfulness.

Sin can cause us to get crusty, but discipline observed
in the lives of others keeps our hearts sensitive to our
potential for compromise. The imperative "to encourage
one another" and to be cautious of the "deceitfulness of
sin" brings the text into the arena of discipline. This
exhortation to mutual encouragement is wise since believers in isolation are more likely to succumb to the subtle
temptations that press in upon them.

The admonition to discipline need not always imply
excommunication. Church discipline in the form of constant, daily encouragement and admonition keeps the fellowship healthy and confirms each believer's responsibility
for other members of the body.

The Purposes of Discipline
for Church Leaders

Leaders in the body of Christ are assigned the task of keeping the church pure and faithful. Church discipline speaks to leaders about their duties to the church and also to members about obedience to their leaders.

A Message to Leaders. In 2 Timothy 4:1-2, Paul charges the young pastor to "correct, rebuke and encourage—with great patience and careful instruction"—those over whom God has given him responsibility. Timothy is charged by God to guide the church in exercising discipline. This is not to be despotic, dictatorial, or legalistic. Rather, all discipline must be done with patience and careful teaching (v. 2).

A Message to the Congregation. Speaking to the congregation about its attitude and responsibility to the leadership, Paul writes in 1 Thessalonians 5:12-13:

> Now we ask you, brothers, to respect those who work hard among you, who are over you in the Lord and who admonish you. Hold them in the highest regard in love because of their work. Live in peace with each other.

The flock of Jesus is responsible to respect their God-ordained leaders. Because of the leaders' Christ-like character, their admonitions will be respected and observed, and they will be esteemed in love. Members of a local church always feel secure and protected by leaders who reflect the nature of Christ, the Head of the church.

Loving, corrective discipline is a major tool in God's Kingdom to assure that a congregation has healthy lines of authority and mutual love and respect. With this in mind, Paul introduces three purposes of discipline for the leadership of any local church.

Purpose 1: To protect the Scriptures from distortion and error.

Stopping Empty Talk (Titus 1:10-14)

In Titus 1, Paul warns Titus about the heretical teachings and scriptural perversions that were emerging in the church in Crete:

> For there are many rebellious people, mere talkers and deceivers, especially those of the circumcision group. They must be silenced, because they are ruining whole households by teaching things they ought not to teach—and that for the sake of dishonest gain. Even one of their own prophets has said, "Cretans are always liars, evil brutes, lazy gluttons." This testimony is true. Therefore, rebuke them sharply, so that they will be sound in the faith and will pay no attention to Jewish myths or to the commands of those who reject the truth.

The primary purpose for church discipline in this case was to protect the Scriptures from distortion and error. Fast action was necessary to put a muzzle on false teaching, and Paul's instruction to "rebuke them sharply" suggests that one confrontation may not suffice. The leadership of the church must protect the integrity of the Word of God, and disciplinary action may at times be necessary for this "truth maintenance."

Purpose 2: To affirm submission to the authority of God and his designated leaders.

Testing the Obedient Spirit (2 Corinthians 2:9; 7:12)

> The reason I wrote you was to see if you would stand the test and be obedient in everything.

So even though I wrote to you, it was not on account of the one who did the wrong or of the injured party, but rather that before God you could see for yourselves how devoted to us you are.

The master church planter, as the chief apostle, was testing the church's submission to his leadership and apostolic commands. Would they obey God's authority as expressed through Paul? How the fellowship responded to his admonition to exercise discipline toward the sinning brother demonstrated their true spirit.

Therefore, one implied purpose of church discipline is the affirmation of a congregation's obedience to the authority of God and his designated leadership. Discipline establishes authority as being from God and worthy of obedience.

Purpose 3: To prove that the leadership loves and cares.

Hopelessly Devoted (2 Corinthians 7:8-9)

Even if I [Paul] caused you sorrow by my letter, I do not regret it. Though I did regret it—I see that my letter hurt you, but only for a little while—yet now I am happy, not because you were made sorry, but because your sorrow led you to repentance. For you became sorrowful as God intended and so were not harmed in any way by us.

Paul is referring to his harsh words in 1 Corinthians 5 about the need for immediate discipline of a sinful brother. He chastized the church because he loved her. He got involved with the discipline because of his genuine care for the Corinthians. Paul always sought the best for the church. He loved the Corinthians and therefore, in both letters, his primary concern was their protection. It was tough love, but it was real.

The leaders of the local ministry must not be afraid to exercise church discipline; on the contrary, they must accept their responsibility to express love and concern *through* discipline. Without the loving exercise of church discipline, the congregation will not be convinced of the leadership's godly care. The leadership of a local ministry should exercise discipline as a statement of genuine love.

A Summary of the Primary Purposes of Corrective Church Discipline

For the Offender:

1. To restore and reconcile the offender to God and the fellowship (Gal. 6:1).

2. To shame the offender leading to restoration to the fellowship and a godly lifestyle (2 Thess. 3:14-15).

3. To destroy fleshly lusts and return the believer to the rule of Christ (1 Cor. 5:1-5).

For the Corporate Body:

1. To purify the worship and message of the church (1 Cor. 5:6-8).

2. To deny the enemy any advantage or access into the church (2 Cor. 2:5-11).

3. To avoid giving God cause to set himself against the local church (Rev. 2:5).

For the Individual Church Member:

1. To assist in strengthening one's faith and maintenance of a clear conscience (1 Tim. 1:18-20).

2. To promote intense self-examination in each church member's life (2 Cor. 7:11).

3. To confirm each believer's responsibility for members of the body (Heb. 3:13).

For Church Leaders:

1. To protect the Scriptures from distortion and error (Titus 1:10-14).

2. To affirm submission to the authority of God and his designated leaders (2 Cor. 2:9; 7:12).

3. To prove that the leadership loves and cares (2 Cor. 7:8-9).

Properly exercised discipline has great value for every Christian involved. But even though a Christian might be convinced of the enormous value of discipline, loving rebuke by the church is little help for the believer who has been emotionally fractured by the moral failure of his spiritual leader or another Christian.

In the next chapter, I offer help for disoriented and crushed Christians to find their way during those confusing times of disappointment. I suggest steps for rebuilding shaken confidence and regaining emotional footing following a disappointment. And in the chapters ahead, I provide a detailed blueprint for exercising this healing art of loving discipline.

Notes

1. James Montgomery Boice, "Galatians," *The Expositor's Bible Commentary*, ed. Frank E. Gaebelein, 12 vols. (Grand Rapids, Mich.: Zondervan Publishing House, 1976), 10:502.

2. Josephus, *Antiquities of the Jews*, e.12.1.

3. A. Harbro Collins, "The Function of 'Excommunication' in Paul," *The Harvard Theological Review* 73 (January/February 1980):253.

4. Edwin L. Adams, "A Study of Corrective Discipline in the Apostolic Church" (Ph.D. diss. Southwestern Baptist Theological Seminary, 1949), 196.

5. R. C. H. Lenski, *The Interpretation of St. Paul's First and Second Epistle to the Corinthians* (Minneapolis: Augsburg Publishing House, 1961), 220-22. Perhaps some physical suffering was sometimes divinely inflicted with a remedial purpose.

6. Oliver Price, "How to Begin Church Discipline," *Moody Monthly*, May 1979, 37.

7. Knuteson, *Calling the Church to Discipline*, 32.

8. Peterson, *Discipline in the Local Church* (Minneapolis: Central Conservative Baptist Theological Seminary Press, n.d.), 19.

PART THREE

Administering First Aid to the Offender

CHAPTER SIX

Truthing It... Step by Step

Distinctiveness is attractive to Americans. Those noteworthy characteristics that set certain people apart are of peculiar interest to us. Seeing John Wayne's last interview with Barbara Walters reminded me that, even three months before his death, he was still very distinctive in the way he spoke, walked, and expressed his flair for life. For some, distinctives can become a trademark.

There is a distinctive that God has called every Christian to accept as a trademark in our relationships with others. It's a distinctive that every Christian should practice when personally offended or when another brother is seen in a wrong.

A Distinctive Savior

One of the greatest distinctives in the life of Christ was the way he confronted others. He was known for speaking the truth, often in a lovingly confrontational way. In the Gospel of John, we find Jesus at the well of Sychar interacting with an adulteress from the village (John 4). After Christ offered the woman water from another world, the conversation went like this:

> "Sir, give me this water so that I won't get thirsty and have to keep coming here to draw water."
>
> He told her, "Go, call your husband and come back."
>
> "I have no husband," she replied.
>
> Jesus said to her, "You are right when you say you have no husband. The fact is, you have had five husbands, and the man you now have is not your husband. What you have just said is quite true" (John 4:15-18).

Notice how firmly Jesus stayed with the hard facts of her unwholesome life. He gently confronted her with the truth.

In his dealings with people, Jesus wore the distinctive of being simple, concise, and truthful. He lived by this philosophy in all his relationships. Being truthful with others is a trademark every Christian needs.

Indistinct Christians

Modern evangelicals have a problem when it comes to speaking truthfully to one another. If we feel the necessity to confront someone, we either respond harshly and destructively, or we break out in hives. We've lost the art of "speaking the truth" with those who have offended us.

Truth, A Badge of Courage

Paul was a truth teller, and he connects the exercise to spiritual maturity:

> . . . until we all reach unity in the faith and in the knowledge of the Son of God and become mature, attaining to the whole measure of the fullness of Christ.
>
> Then we will no longer be infants, tossed back and forth by the waves, and blown here and there by every wind of teaching and by the cunning and craftiness of men in their deceitful scheming. Instead, speaking the truth in love, we will in all things grow up into him who is the Head, that is, Christ (Eph. 4:13-15).

Speaking the truth in love takes maturity; it also develops maturity. It is a vital part of discipleship and a badge of distinction every believer should wear. Let me put it in "Monday morning" terms with two illustrations.

Chet has been an employee with the company for as long as you. His work area is adjacent to yours. One Monday morning, you are told by your coworkers that Chet has been spreading gossip about you and the quality of your work. To make matters worse, you have been shunned by Chet at the coffee pot many times over the last few weeks. There is tension. You're offended and angry, and rightly so. The hurt goes even deeper since Chet is a Christian who faithfully sits in the same sanctuary with you on Sundays. How should you handle the offense?

It is a rainy Thursday afternoon. You've just dropped

off your children at a friend's house for a birthday party when you decide to make a last-minute stop at the grocery store. As you stand in the checkout line, you notice that your pastor and an unfamiliar lady have just come out of the travel agent's office next door and are chatting in the parking lot. Then the pastor kisses the woman, opens her car door, and waves good-bye. You're shocked! *What sin has my spiritual leader fallen into? Who do I need to tell? What should I do?*

What is our normal response to situations such as these? Over the years, I've observed five ways we tend to respond. *Only one is correct!*

Our Normal Responses

The first common response to our hurt is the *"I'll get even"* response. "I'm going to talk to the boss and get Chet's job, or at least I'm going to retaliate by discussing his faulty character with his friends." In the case of the philandering pastor, a "get even" response may be, "I'll salve my disappointment, hurt, and confusion by hinting to others that our pastor is having an affair."

This attitude reveals a wrong motivation. When we're concerned only about getting even or putting someone in his place, we are selfishly motivated. We demonstrate that neither the other person nor our relationship with him is very valuable. I am amazed how many believers resort to this tactic because of their hurt, but this response shows no Christ-like maturity. It's destructive and should be avoided.

The *"It's hopeless, and I don't care"* response is also typical. It's a "conflicts are to be avoided at all costs" frame of mind. The one who feels this way thinks to himself, "This situation is so uncomfortable that I'm going to sweep it under the rug. Besides, they're not going to change anyway." The outcome of this response is almost always emotional indigestion. Since the problem is not confronted, the inner feelings pile up like compost. In his book, *Caring Enough to Confront*, David Augsberger explains how unproductive this response is:

> It is a way out of conflict, not a way through. And a way out is no way at all.
>
> In this lose-lose stance everyone loses. There is no risk of power, no trusting love. "Show me to the nearest exit," the person requests over the shoulder.[1]

Many hide behind a third option which I call the *"I'll smile through my teeth"* response. I confess this is my personal reaction when offended. It's a more internalized and pragmatic response.[2] "I'll yield to this conflict with Chet because I need his help and his contact in the office." Or, "I'll not mention what I saw in the parking lot, because I need the pastor to love me as a person. I hate to have anyone angry at me." Those who have this response would rather keep their job and feel like a frustrated doormat than address the problem head on with dignity.

Fourth, Christians often hide their feelings behind a *"forgive and forget"* attitude. "It's wrong for me to judge others. I've been guilty of a few errors in my life, too! Who am I to point a finger?" In the next chapter, I will address the problem of judging others. However, the real danger lies within the heart of the offended. His emotional temperature rises every time the other person's name is mentioned. While churning inside, he continues to act as though nothing is wrong. He smiles and remains silent, but it's a silence both dangerous and destructive.

If "getting even," "giving up," or "simply enduring" is not the right response, then how should we respond? Every Christian should *speak the truth in love* (Eph. 4:15). We realize, "We are both people of integrity; therefore this problem should be addressed. I have been offended [or I have watched what seems to be an offensive act], and in my anger I need to speak the truth." The Christian who responds like this has the maturity to see the conflict as something needing godly attention. This response is the truly caring and loving way to approach any offense or sin in another's life.

> Truthing it is trusting others with my actual feelings. . . . Avoiding honest statements of real feelings and viewpoints is often considered kindness, thoughtfulness, or generosity. More often it is the most cruel thing I can do to others. It is a kind of benevolent lying.[3]

What do you do when you're offended and justifiably angry or hurt? Do you know how to "truth it"? Are you mature enough to wear this bold New Testament badge of distinctiveness?

The Master's Model

In Matthew 18, the One who is the Truth gives the proper steps for approaching another in truth. The procedure he lays out can have a revolutionary impact on all your relationships, whether they be with a pastor, another Christian, or even a non-Christian. If exercised properly, these biblical steps can renovate many of your difficult struggles with those who have disappointed you.

The first thing a Christian *must* do when offended is go personally to the one guilty of the offense. In Matthew 18:15, Jesus informs us:

> If your brother sins against you, go and show
> him his fault, just between the two of you. If he
> listens to you, you have won your brother over.

Jesus has two categories of offenders in mind: those who offend us directly (such as Chet), and those who have been involved in sin or in some way offended the integrity of the believing community (such as the pastor caught with another woman). Christ's words would make little sense if we were called on to speak the truth only to those who had personally and privately offended us. That would mean a nonbeliever or a Christian from another church would be off limits. We would never be able to clear up our conflicts, because the offending brother was outside our church fellowship. Also, the leaders of the church would be handicapped. Christ's words would restrict them from speaking the truth to anyone other than those who offended them personally. Clearing up conflicts between other Christians within the church body would be impossible.

The first step is to be taken against *any* sin, whether it touches your life personally or the life of the corporate body. Whether it be Chet, your pastor, or some believer involved in improper business ethics, lying, mishandling of finances, or immorality, you need to go. Even if the offense is not against you personally . . . go!

Sore Toes Must Go!

Jesus' command to go catches me flatfooted. If I'm not the one who has done the wrong, why should I be the one to initiate clearing it up? Why doesn't the offender come to me?

The reasons are not hard to understand. Perhaps the other person doesn't know he has committed a wrong.

Perhaps he is not guilty, but we perceive the situation or the facts wrongly. If he is guilty, he may be building up sinful offenses in God's eyes, a serious problem that must be confronted as soon as possible. For the spiritual well-being of both the offended and the offender, an attempt to address the problem and seek reconciliation needs to be initiated by the wounded as soon as possible. It's a wonderful tactic that righteous people should follow.

Saying that it is the responsibility of the offended to go to the wrongdoer does not mean the wrongdoer is not accountable to God. In Matthew 5:23-24, Jesus speaks to the offender who is trying to worship but has not been reconciled to the one he has harmed:

> "Therefore, if you are offering your gift at the altar and there remember that your brother has something against you, leave your gift there in front of the altar. First go and be reconciled to your brother; then come and offer your gift."

The offender is also responsible! Good relationships are a prerequisite to worship, and both parties are obligated to seek reconciliation. "When discord between believers takes place, ideally they ought to meet each other on the way to one another's house to seek reconciliation."[4] However, the violated one should never hold back, but go first if necessary.

Now that we know to *whom* we should speak the truth, Jesus tells us *why*.

Accomplish What?

Next, Jesus reveals the specific purpose for the face-to-face visit. It's "to show him his fault." Jesus has in mind an approach that is *tentative* and *gracious*. Rather than a harsh rebuke, a gracious discussion of the facts as they have been observed is the proper spirit. Jay Adams describes this proper attitude:

> That is to say, he first goes and explains the situation as he has perceived or experienced it, saying something like this: "As far as I can see, you have wronged me in such and such a way, but if you have an explanation, I am ready to hear it before passing final judgment."[5]

Beware of Magnifying Glasses

Our Lord's instruction doesn't encourage us to take a magnifying glass to every Christian's private life. I'm not obligated to look for hidden spiritual compromises in others. I'm required only to deal with problems that come to my attention and that are obviously in need of confrontation.

Also, dredging up petty differences or every personal disagreement is not in the mind of Christ. Proverbs reminds us that "love covers over all wrongs" (10:12) and "to overlook an offense" is a glorious thing (19:11). Petty differences are to be washed away by love. They should be forgiven and overlooked. The Christian is always to be quick to forgive, giving the benefit of the doubt.

In light of the soft approach to the first step of speaking the truth and the reminder to overlook insignificant offenses, when do we know that an offense must be addressed? What triggers my need to confront another?

When I am hurt by another, I usually try to overlook the offense out of love. But sometimes the problems are too big and painful. I've learned that issues need to be confronted whenever there seems to be an irreconcilable barrier between me and the offender. When I struggle with a bad attitude toward another, it invariably comes to my mind during my morning shower. I find myself cleaning my outside but muddying my inside. After a few showers spent replaying the offense, I realize the problem is not just a small, forgettable rub, but worthy of speaking the truth in love. I like how one author explains it:

> That is to say, any matter which is carried over to another day, any matter which makes you feel different toward that person for more than a passing moment, any matter that throws love's covers off must be brought up.[6]

In addition, if you see a brother or sister losing a wrestling match with sin, that's a green light to go! When a Christian's character or the integrity of a Christian community is impugned, it is the responsibility of every believer to lovingly address the problem.

Both Chet and the pastor need to experience step one of the "speaking the truth" process. But how should the interview be held? How can we approach Chet or the pastor without causing great damage? How can we do it in a way that keeps us from sinning ourselves?

Approached How?

In Matthew 18:15, Jesus gives the secret to the proper handling of loving confrontation. The initial confrontation is to be "just between the two of you," a one-on-one encounter of the very private kind. If done the Lord's way, there will be protection from several common mistakes.

The one-on-one approach *protects against sinful gossip*. The responsibility to go solo pushes the offended in the direction of the wrongdoer and not toward other brothers or sisters who might be prone to spread gossip or cause character defamation. Before speaking of the offense or even seeking counsel from others, we should go to the errant brother. There are many biblical prohibitions against idle talk and destructive gossip, and Jesus desires to keep us from sin.

Also, sitting alone, across the table from the one who has inflicted the damage, is a much easier atmosphere for explanations. The possibility of misunderstanding the details and circumstances behind the offense are greatly increased when this step is not taken. In fact, often the accusations are false! Going straight to the source of the problem without spreading damaging gossip *allows for an explanation and resolution without further damage.*

Also, if handled properly, an environment of caring is established so that if the accusation proves to be true, *repentance and reconciliation can take place quickly and more easily.* Forgiveness can be given and the matter resolved.

The Lord knew how to resolve personal bruises the right way. The directive to go immediately, face to face, avoids many of the damaging schemes our hearts can cook up. Our avoidance mentality is always scheming up a less confrontational way to deal with hurt. I know of Christians who have drafted letters of accusations. I've even heard of some who had special authority over the wrongdoer (i.e., a boss) who initiated a power play by moving all subordinates into his office and rebuking the offender openly.

There are so many ways the situation could be mis-handled, but the Lord's way is the right way. And, as we should expect, he is consistent, for at the judgment seat, the eternal Judge, Jesus himself, will treat each of us with the same respect—one-on-one, in love (2 Cor. 5:10).

Having the proper attitude in a close-quarters confrontation is important. This proper attitude is seen in the context of the whole chapter of Matthew 18. The first four verses discuss the necessity for humility in the kingdom of God. Verses 5-11 deal with those who sin and draw others into their offense. Verses 12-14, the lost sheep parable, reveal how God feels about those of his fold who willfully go astray. They need to be sought out and returned! Verses 15-20 tell us how to retrieve the disobedient sheep. Then the chapter ends with an amazing lesson delivered to Peter. The parable of the unmerciful servant makes it clear that the Christian's attitude in the midst of personal hurt should be one of *unlimited forgiveness*.

The context surrounding the Lord's directive tells us that he wants us to approach the hurt with restoration in mind, with love in our hearts, moving into the confrontation with caution. Forgiveness and reconciliation are the goal. We must always be willing to give the offender the benefit of the doubt.

Awareness of the Outcome

Let's assume you've made the necessary arrangement to have a face-to-face meeting with Chet (or you've called the church office and set up an appointment with your pastor). You have not been guilty of spreading rumors or making false accusations. You know there will be tension in the air, but you're confident you've handled the situation properly. What could you expect as possible responses?

Jesus mentions two possible outcomes from the meeting. The first is positive: "If he listens to you, you have won your brother over." If he hears your complaint and responds in a godly manner, there should be repentance and forgiveness bringing the issue to closure. If Chet admits his guilt and asks for forgiveness, your emotional hurt should be dropped. You may learn that he is *innocent*, that he was guilty only of being outspoken about a work-related project, an attitude that would hardly be considered slander. How that would clear the air!

Either way, "you have won your brother over." The friendship can be restored, the issue buried. If sin is involved, forgiveness is needed and can be freely given. Once forgiveness is given, the problem must not be dredged up again or discussed with others. Since it has been handled Christ's way, we can stop brooding over the hurt and start loving again.

The other possible outcome is not so positive. The offender may respond to your one-on-one confrontation by refusing to listen. What then?

Truth-It . . . Step Two

If the one-on-one confrontation does not bring a resolution, then verse 16 is the second step the Lord considers necessary to speak the truth properly. If Chet admits he is guilty but is unwilling to reconcile, this next step should be taken:

"But if he will not listen, take one or two others along, so that 'every matter may be established by the testimony of two or three witnesses.' "

Do not assume that because you have followed the Lord's blueprint the outcome of the meeting will be like a fairy tale. Often the person confronted is in denial or dealing with personal baggage that could hinder the healing. Nevertheless, we must do what's right.

The first step may involve several attempts before it

becomes painfully obvious that the offender has no intention of changing. Then more severe action must be taken. But if the offender demonstrates some openness, even though he may not be willing to repent just yet, then another one-on-one discussion may be needed.

A Little Help from My Friends

At what point do I take others to help confront the offender? Jesus doesn't leave any room for guessing: "If he will not listen," then we bring others into the process. After failed face-to-face attempts, the disciple is to be accompanied by "one or two" witnesses.

Certain contextual clues help us understand why Christ wanted witnesses present. The first clue is found in the second half of verse 16, where the Lord quotes from Deuteronomy 19; this chapter, beginning with verse 15, deals with disputes within the spiritual community of Israel. The Mosaic code demanded adequate testimony against any Israelite accused of sin before a judge. Jesus draws on the Old Testament prohibition that a person may not be convicted of a crime on the basis of a single witness (Num. 35:30; Deut. 17:6; 19:15). At least two witnesses are necessary to insure that an accusation is done with integrity, truthfulness, and in an unprejudiced manner.

By citing this Old Testament provision, is Jesus demanding that the witnesses be *eyewitnesses* to the offense?

> Matthew leaves no indication that the one or two others shall have witnessed the sin committed against the one who takes them along. Therefore their going does not have the purpose of establishing the original charge (the truth of which is taken for granted) . . . but of strengthening

the reproof with a view toward restoration.[7]

The witnesses are called upon both to bring moral pressure upon the offender and to observe his attitude if it should become necessary to testify before the church. The witnesses are to assist in the attempted restoration of the errant brother, but if the attempt fails they will serve as witnesses not of the original transgression but of the failure to repent.

Bringing a sin to a brother's attention in the presence of witnesses may sound threatening or intimidating. Yet Jesus' purpose is not to threaten or intimidate the sinner into repentance, but to help him realize the seriousness of his sin. As one pastor remarked, "Although moving into the group process is scary, it does improve the attention level."[8]

Two of the Most Important Steps in Your Life

Let's review. We have taken an in-depth look at the divine directive to lovingly confront one who has sinned against us or is involved in an offense that breaks his Christian witness. The harmed Christian brother or sister must take the initial responsibility to address the problem.

Step two is to be taken when the offender refuses to repent after the one-on-one confrontation. Jesus commands that two or more witnesses accompany the disciple so that moral influence will be brought to bear and that by the mouths of the witnesses the facts may be confirmed.

Advice for Truthing It

Confronting another believer is never easy, but there are some tips that can help make a tough experience more successful and loving. I use them constantly. They're worth committing to memory before you march into any confrontation.

113

First, *express your love before you express your problem.* Proverbs 10:12 reminds us, "Hatred stirs up dissension, but love covers over all wrongs." You must always let the other person know that you genuinely care for him. Even though there may be anger, you must express personal concern. You *can* be angry with a person and love him at the same time.

> A context of caring must come before confrontation. A sense of support must be present before criticism. An experience of empathy must precede evaluation.[9]

This keeps unnecessary barriers from rising up and blocking your desire to settle the issue.

Second, *avoid asking inflammatory questions.* Asking "Why?" is like tossing gasoline on a fire. Questions such as, "Why are you wanting to hurt my reputation?" put you in an adversarial situation. By asking "Why?" we set ourselves up as judge and jury of the offender's actions. Pointing the finger of accusation is unnecessary and harmful. You've come to reconcile a relationship by lovingly confronting sin; *accusing* is out of bounds.

Third, *keep the focus on you.* Healthy portions of the word *I* will do wonders for the confrontation. In most cases, you are meeting with the errant brother to express your feelings, needs, hurts, concerns, or observations about his behavior. Therefore, use *I* to preface your statements.

I recently had a recurring problem with a fellow Christian. In our face-to-face confrontation, I explained, "I am concerned over the way certain responsibilities have been handled." This approach was much better received than if I had said, "You make me angry because you consistently fail to fulfill your responsibilities." "I" statements keep the focus on us.

"You messages" are most often attacks, criticisms, devaluations of the other person, labels, or ways of fixing blame. "I messages" are clear, honest, confessional. "I messages" own my anger, my responsibility, my demands without placing blame.[10]

Fourth, *be simple and factual.* It is imperative that the facts are put forth graciously. When we confront, anger and hurt can wedge into our motives. One of the most powerful tools available in such difficult times is *silence.* We are often frightened by silence in our communication with people, but stating the facts and silently waiting for a response will often allow God's Spirit to work amazing results. Proverbs 10:19 reminds us, "When words are many, sin is not absent, but he who holds his tongue is wise."

Finally, *be clear about the response you're expecting.* What do you want from them? State your expectation: "I want to rebuild our relationship," or "I want you to repent of your sins and turn back to God," or even, "I want you to apologize for slandering me." Tell the errant brother what you want, and then be silent as you await his response. Watch what God does in the situation. If he is innocent or if he is guilty and repents, "you have won your brother over." Whatever his response, you have sought the best for both of you, God's way.

The Value of Tough Love

Let's face it, most Christians are afraid to confront another believer's sin. However, both Jesus and Paul called every follower of Christ to see speaking the truth in love as a valuable part of the Christian growth experience. We are commanded to be rightly related to every one in the body of Christ: "If it is possible, as far as it depends on you, live at peace with everyone" (Rom. 12:18).

If Christians had been speaking the truth in love, fewer ministers of the gospel would be in prison today. Many churches would still be proclaiming the gospel to the glory of Christ. Christians across this country would be actively involved in their local fellowships rather than living isolated lives in bitterness and devastation. Someone could have taken Christ's words seriously and stopped moral disasters before they made major shockwaves.

I'm convinced a large percentage of believers have someone they need to approach, but they've allowed the infection to spread until it's irreparable. Some of us need to start speaking the truth . . . *today.* Maybe there is someone you need to approach this week. If you will, you may have the joy of watching many of the log-jammed relationships in your life break free.

By the way, the pastor seen kissing a strange woman in the parking lot received step one of the discipline process. That lady he kissed . . . was his sister! He had accompanied her to the travel agent to pick up tickets for her return flight to New York. If this situation had not been handled Christ's way, who knows what the outcome might have been.

If we're honest about our feelings, the fear of being judgmental and condescending often keeps us from doing what is right. We find ourselves in a confusing predicament.

116

We are commanded to confront in love, but we are also commanded to refrain from judging others. After all, it was Jesus who said, "Do not judge!" Is it ever okay to pass judgment on another? Isn't it a contradiction to be a Christian and judgmental? How can this tension be resolved?

Notes

1. David Augsberger, *Caring Enough to Confront*, rev. ed. (Ventura, Calif.: Regal Books, 1981), 14.

2. Ibid., 14.

3. Ibid., 27.

4. Jay Adams, *Handbook of Church Discipline* (Grand Rapids, Mich.: Zondervan Publishing House), 49.

5. Ibid., 50.

6. Ibid., 55.

7. Robert H. Gundry, *Matthew: A Commentary on His Literary and Theological Art* (Grand Rapids, Mich.: Wm. B. Eerdmans Publishing Co., 1982), 368.

8. Donald L. Bubna, "Redemptive Love: The Key to Church Discipline," *Leadership Journal* 2 (Summer 1981):81.

9. Augsberger, *Caring Enough to Confront*, 52.

10. Ibid., 42.

CHAPTER SEVEN

To Judge or Not to Judge, Isn't That the Question?

"To be, or not to be: that is the question."

This one famous line from *Hamlet* almost exhausts my knowledge of Shakespeare's works. Actually, I shouldn't be quite so hard on myself. Now and then, around the dinner table, I have been known to speak with a little Shakespearean flavor—"To eat or not to eat, there is *no* question!"

Everyone Knows It's Wrong!

Perhaps the most quoted verse in the Bible is Matthew 7:1, "Do not judge, or you too will be judged." Paul Engle describes a typical setting in which the verse might be used:

Jennifer's church friends gently supported her during her traumatic transition back to single-hood, but they couldn't help her ward off the pangs of loneliness the attractive divorcée felt as she returned to her empty condominium each night. They watched as she responded to Bob, a married employee of a Christian parachurch organization. Their casual luncheon appointments led to a serious affair. "It's none of our business," one of her friends said. "What they do is between themselves and the Lord." Another said, "We especially don't want to offend her. She might give up teaching her Sunday school class. And besides, who are we to pass judgment?"[1]

This all too common tragedy sets up the real-life question, Should a Christian judge another? In the previous chapter, we discovered that Jesus calls every Christian to be a sensitive, cautious judge of another's life when necessary. But doesn't Jesus contradict himself when he calls Christians to confront a sinning brother in Matthew 18:15-16 and then commands us *not* to be judgmental in Matthew 7:1? When is judging right, and when is it wrong? On the subject of judging others, several observations can be made.

First, Christians can be very judgmental people. Surely by now you know this to be true. We are guilty of judging each other at almost every level. We have judgmental thoughts about how others educate their children, whether public, private, or home school. We judge what others eat, drink, and do (Rom. 14:1-12). We judge their level of success, their clothes, their spiritual commitment, their friends, their habits, even their personalities. We are at heart a judgmental people. And worse, we like doing it.

Second, judging others is unavoidable. How can any human go through life without making judgments? We cannot give up our critical faculties or our responsibility to discern and appraise. We must not suspend the ability to make a value judgment about what is right and wrong. Judging or criticizing of this nature is a necessary part of our lives.

Maybe you were blessed with a grandmother like mine. I can still remember her scolding me, "If you can't say something positive about someone, don't say anything at all." However, as I have experienced a little of life's complications, I'm no longer sure she was entirely right.

Take, for instance, the neurosurgeon in San Diego who made several serious slips with his scalpel during routine surgeries in the early 1970s. He had been taking drugs and was liable for his actions. When the crimes surfaced, he fled and started a practice in another state where he once again repeated his mistakes. If this surgeon were to move to your town and you became aware of his past record the day before your neighbor was to have surgery, would you take my grandmother's advice? The truth is, Christians today really don't know when it's okay to judge and when it is not. "To judge or not to judge" is a great question.

The only way confusion can be removed and the apparent contradiction settled is to carefully examine God's Word. And there is more than enough evidence to examine since judging is one of the most mentioned subjects in the New Testament. In the pages ahead we will participate in an old-fashioned Bible study covering the three most significant passages on judging. James, Jesus, and Paul have much to say about the Christian's responsibility to judge.

The Elder James

James was a powerful man of God, and when he spoke the congregation listened. On the subject of judging others, he is unequivocal:

> Brothers, do not slander one another. Anyone who speaks against his brother or judges him speaks against the law and judges it. When you judge the law, you are not keeping it, but sitting in judgment on it. There is only one Lawgiver and Judge, the one who is able to save and destroy. But you—who are you to judge your neighbor? (James 4:11-12).

At first glance it looks as if James flatly says, "Never judge!" But wait a moment. Did you notice that the elder's words are surrounded by a context dealing with the law? What is James trying to communicate?

Too Much Tongue, Not Enough Heart

Two words in these verses reveal the type of judging James is speaking against. The verbs *judge* and *slander* are connected in his mind, and we know that slander, or "speaking evil against" someone, is never condoned in Scripture. Paul uses *slander* in Titus 2:3 to refer to those who find fault with others and pass their criticisms on to the church. In a perverted and sinful sense, this is a judging spirit.

Through James's eyes we see the act of judgmentally condemning another coupled with slander. James is not condemning judging others' sins nor is he contradicting the Lord's call to speak the truth to one another. Rather he is speaking out against one Christian belittling another. It is wrong to slander or attack another person's character.

A critical heart is betrayed by condescending lips.

James's reference to God being the only judge tips us off as to the motivation of the slanderer's heart. The sole motivation for the censure of a fellow believer was to give the slanderer that "superior spirit" by passing along negative evaluations of another. James was condemning too much tongue and not enough heart on the part of some in the church. Putting someone else down in order to elevate ourselves, acting as judge over another's life, is sin.

Psalm 101:5 speaks against anyone who participates in improper judgment and slander of another:

> Whoever slanders his neighbor in secret,
>   him will I put to silence;
> whoever has haughty eyes and a proud heart,
>   him will I not endure.

Symptoms of a Judgmental Spirit

James is not speaking against judging or confronting those who are in sin or who have offended you. Rather he is condemning a judgmental spirit prone to backbiting, speaking critically, passing sentence on others. This form of judging is ugly and expressly prohibited by the elder.

But how do you detect a judgmental spirit of the ungodly kind? A Christian with such a spirit will have an improved opinion of himself when the one he is judging falls. The inner voice might say, "Oh good, they've failed. They've made a mistake, and I feel so much better." If another's failure improves your opinion of yourself, a judgmental spirit is present within you!

Another sign of a judgmental spirit is seen when a Christian desires to see another punished. When the "Pearlygate" scandals hit the front pages in the late 1980s,

I heard many Christians respond with glee to the sentencing of the televangelists. "Great! They deserve it! Sixty years in prison would not be enough to pay them back for all the hurt they have caused."

Other indicators of a slandering, judgmental spirit are all too common. We know we have a judgmental spirit if we are eager to spread the bad news of someone else's failure ("Did you hear about so-and-so?"). We know we have a judgmental spirit if another's failure prompts us to rehearse his past failures and say, "Well, I'm not surprised." We know we have a judgmental spirit if another's failures cause hardness of heart toward him and an unwillingness to forgive.

> A little seed lay on the ground
>   and soon began to sprout.
> Now which of all the flowers around
>   it mused, shall I come out?
> The lily's face is fair and proud
>   but just a trifle cold:
> The rose, I think, is rather loud
>   and then its fashion old.
> The violet is all very well
>   but not a flower I'd choose,
> Nor yet a canterbury bell;
>   I never cared for blues.
> And so it criticized and judged each flower,
>   this supercilious seed,
> Until it woke one summer hour
>   and found itself a weed.
>   (Author unknown)

The elder's prohibition against judging others doesn't contradict the command of Christ to speak the truth in love when someone needs it. Rather it speaks against those with a slanderous, judgmental attitude who seek to hurt another and, ultimately, destroy the unity of the church.

But what about the words of Jesus in Matthew 7:1? Do they contradict his later teaching about the proper exercise of discipline?

The Lord Jesus

In Matthew 7:1-5, Jesus declared:

> "Do not judge, or you too will be judged. For in the same way you judge others, you will be judged, and with the measure you use, it will be measured to you.

> "Why do you look at the speck of sawdust in your brother's eye and pay no attention to the plank in your own eye? How can you say to your brother, 'Let me take the speck out of your eye,' when all the time there is a plank in your own eye? You hypocrite, first take the plank out of your own eye, and then you will see clearly to remove the speck from your brother's eye."

The Boomerang Principle

Jesus begins his teaching just as James did. He stands firmly against the Christian setting himself up as judge over another. However, Jesus' statement includes additional information that suggests he has something different in mind.

When Jesus says, "For in the *same way* you judge others, you will be judged, and with the *measure* you use, it will be measured to you," he has in mind a peculiar biblical truth. I call it the Boomerang Effect: when we judge others, that same spirit of judgment will boomerang on us. God will judge those who judge others, and he will do it using *their* measuring rod. If we are harsh in our judgment of others, God will be equally harsh with us. He watches the measuring tool and uses its duplicate in his judgments.

This biblical principle operates on a corporate level as well. That is, the judgment comes back to the offender through those around him. I have watched people withdraw from a harsh, judgmental person. Jesus said this would happen; it's God's form of punishment. God will judge, and others will judge as well through their willful withdrawing from the offender. A critical spirit harms the offender more than it harms those under attack. It boomerangs on us!

The penalty for judging others seems so severe that we might ask, Is Jesus suggesting that Christians just leave each other alone? Is he promoting a live-and-let-live policy? A closer look at the next few verses will show that the problem is not judging others, but the failure to judge *ourselves* first.

Unqualified Spiritual Ophthalmologists

In verses 3-5, Jesus gives us an amazing visual illustration. Two believers have foreign bodies stuck in their eyes—one a "speck of sawdust," the other a "plank." The speck of sawdust is small and hard to see, but somehow the judgmental brother has noticed it hidden under his brother's lid. The plank, by comparison, is a railroad tie or a telephone pole lodged in the eye of the judgmental person.

The symbolism is striking. Jesus is teaching that when a Christian goes to someone to confront his fault (speck of sawdust) before removing the obstruction in his own

126

vision (a plank), he is blinded. The brother with the judg-mental spirit sees the other's sin but either can't see or ignores his own. His spiritual vision is blocked, blinding him to his own sins and inadequacies . . . especially when they are the same sins he condemns in another!

It's a simple spiritual truth: A Christian must take care of his own faults before addressing the sins of another. We should never set ourselves up as a judge of a brother's failings without first recognizing and judging our own. We cannot be blinded by our own sins and be in a position to help others. Jesus is not demanding sin-less perfection, but sin awareness in our lives (1 John 1:8). Acknowledging and confessing our sins puts us back in the right relationship to lovingly address another (1 John 1:9).

But make no mistake, both foreign bodies must be removed. Jesus doesn't let us assume for a moment that either the plank or the sawdust should be allowed to become permanent obstructions. Not at all. The ideal solution is that both are removed with loving care.

This is the best example in the New Testament of how hypocrites act and think, and Jesus confronts them, calling a spade a spade, "You hypocrite . . ." A hypocrite judges by a different standard than the one he uses to measure his own life. He employs a double standard, liv-ing his life one way and judging by another (Matt. 7:5).

Jesus did not say *never* judge. He even implies that we *should* judge others when he says, "First take the plank out of your eye, and then . . . remove the speck from your brother's eye." Self-evaluation and cleansing are musts before we confront others about their shortcomings. Otherwise, we become hypocrites. So, how should we interpret the teachings of Jesus? Should we judge or not judge? What would Jesus say?

Yes and no. *Yes*, if I first thoroughly examine myself before approaching the other brother. *No*, if the sin problems in my life are not addressed before I confront the sin problems in the offender.

The Apostle Paul

To judge, or not to judge? Paul gives a resounding *yes*! The Christian is absolutely responsible to lovingly and gently judge the sins that are apparent in other's lives. You see, Paul embraced and practiced the biblical mandate Jesus taught in Matthew 18.

A Call to the Spiritual

However, Paul gives the responsibility to judge to "spiritual" Christians. Not everyone is qualified.

> Brothers, if someone is caught in a sin, you who are spiritual should restore him gently. But watch yourself, or you also may be tempted (Gal. 6:1).

A spiritual believer is one who has removed the plank from his own eye before attempting to help a brother or sister remove the sawdust from theirs. Only the spiritually mature are charged with the tough job of speaking the truth in love. This protects a church against hypocritical judges.

I know what you're thinking: "I'll never be spiritual enough to confront another brother." However, spirituality is a matter of self-evaluation and moment-by-moment relationship with Christ. Actually, we are now responsible for two people—ourselves, through self-examination, and also our brother. We cannot be a "live-and-let-live" people. It is selfish not to be involved in helping others through their struggles.

Keep Your Own House Clean

Paul's greatest emphasis is not, Should Christians judge? but, Who should we judge? He commands Christians to judge those *in the church* (Christians), and not to judge those who are nonbelievers (1 Cor. 5:12b). Sadly, many Christians have these two mandates backwards. We can be highly judgmental of those who have no faith in Christ but overlook the blatant rebellion in the person in the pew across the aisle. As God's people, we are never to judge the world; we are to judge the influence of the world *inside the church.*

The Right and Wrong of Judging

There is a proper and helpful way of judging (1 Cor. 5:3-4, 11-12) and an improper, hurtful way of judging (James 4:11; Matt. 7:1-5). You might say the Scriptures both command Christians to judge and at the same time forbid it. Below I have listed the biblical limitations and qualifications that accompany the practice of judging another's life and actions. Should we judge?

> *Yes,* if a fellow believer is involved in sin against us or sin that harms his testimony or the witness of the church.
>
> *Yes,* if the one who needs correction is a Christian (1 Cor. 5:12).
>
> *Yes,* if the confronting is done only after self-evaluation and spiritual preparation, through removal of our own "planks" (Matt. 7:1-5; Gal. 6:1).

129

Yes, if we can confront not with a condemning, slanderous spirit but with a desire for restoration through gentleness and love (James 4:11-12; Gal.6:1-2).

Our spiritual fiber, the level of our maturity as God's people, effectively answers the "to judge or not to judge" question. The call to address sin in another's life can be obeyed only when we ourselves are qualified.

Crawfish Christians

The crawfish is a peculiar creature. God designed it without a backbone; its hard-shell exterior protects vital areas while supporting the body. It's easy for us to become crawfish Christians with a hard outer shell that prevents those who have needs and hurts from penetrating our lives. We don't go out to confront another's problems, nor do we allow others inside our shells.

The New Testament forbids any believer from living this way. As God's people, we are to have the backbone to confront wrong in our lives and in the lives of those in the church. At the same time, we are to be sensitive and approachable. Our strength is to come from within, not from without. Corrective discipline is the internal backbone that supports the body of Christ, but it must be exercised with tenderness, mercy, and grace.

The Best Plans of God and Man

In chapter 6, we looked at the first two steps for confronting wrong in another's life. But what if we exercise our responsibility properly, and our brother's response is not what we had hoped? What if the best laid plans of God and man don't succeed in restoration or repentance? What if steps one and two *both* fail? Jesus gives a tough but effective contingency plan in Matthew 18:17.

Notes

1. Paul Engle, "When It's Okay to Pass Judgment," *Moody Monthly*, May 1981, 37-39.

PART FOUR

Administering First Aid to and through the Church

CHAPTER EIGHT

Truthing It...
Steps Three and Four:
Coming to Grips with Family Affairs

Wrestling with confrontation and discipline in the life of another believer can be difficult. Just to be sure some of the New Testament teaching has soaked in, how about a short pop quiz? The answers are provided at the end of the chapter.

1. Jesus is most concerned that your church be:
   a) debt free
   b) full
   c) pure

2. The apostle Paul exhibited strong disapproval and anger when he:
   a) stubbed his toe on the steps of the Parthenon
   b) found that John Mark abandoned him on

his first missionary journey

    c) found the church had a lax attitude toward sin in its presence

3. If a church wants peace, unity, order, and spiritual maturity, it must have:

    a) a church without any people, with locked doors and empty pews

    b) a coed softball team

    c) a congregation that will rightly administer truth in love

4. The world sneers at the church and ridicules our faith because:

    a) the deacons aren't wearing ties in the worship service

    b) of the televangelist scandals

    c) there is as much wrongdoing in the church as there is in the world

5. If a fellow Christian is involved in sin, you should:

    a) forget it and look the other way (after all, it's none of your business)

    b) judge him and then pass it on to the community gossip

    c) do what Jesus instructed: go to him alone and speak the truth

6. The two most frequently connected words in all the Bible are:

    a) stop that

    b) holy cow

    c) one another

A Family Affair

Our examination of Matthew 18:15-16 has revealed every believer's responsibility to address sin in his own and other Christians' lives. Whether the offense is personal or an action unbecoming to one of God's people, it needs to be addressed in love. In these two verses, Jesus has given us a process for mending relationships and keeping the church pure. The process even works with those outside the church. It's the proper way to handle every relationship problem in life. But what is to happen if the first two steps of the process fail?

Harry was one of the best woodcraftsmen in the area, but work was always hard to find, especially work that would pay what he felt his time and skill were worth. Money was so tight that his wife and son moved in with Harry's parents. It was an unsettling, belittling atmosphere that further reduced Harry's self-esteem, and the marriage began to unravel. During this vulnerable period, Harry found a job out of the city, a job that took him from his family several days a week. Before long Harry was involved in a sexually compromising relationship.

In a few weeks, Harry's Christian brothers had caught on to his persistent absence from the men's studies and church worship. His closest friend confronted him in private, without response. Harry's excuses were typical: he blamed his wife and ten years of confining, pressure-filled marriage. After several months, Harry's friend and a couple of other men from the church met with him, once again to be rejected. Then Harry filed for divorce. A final time, these men confronted Harry about his adultery and divorce, only to be rebuffed.

Jesus knew that a contingency plan would be needed in some cases to fully accomplish repentance and restoration.

In verse 17, he describes steps three and four in which the conflict becomes a family affair.

> "If he refuses to listen to them, tell it to the church; and if he refuses to listen even to the church, treat him as you would a pagan or a tax collector."

In what seems to be a simple procedure, a great force of spiritual pressure is brought to bear on the offender.

Moving to Step Three

Jesus' statement, "if he refuses to listen to them," tells us when step two ends and step three begins. The errant brother or sister has a hardened attitude even after adequate proof of his offense has been given. He will no longer meet with the two or three who confronted him in love; he will neither acknowledge his wrongdoing nor repent. The next step is to tell it to the fellowship.

Tell It to the Family

It is hard to come to grips with the command, "tell it to the church," for it raises two tough questions: Does Jesus want the whole church brought into the process? And, realistically, how can it be done with effectiveness?

Let's assume that come Sunday morning Harry is sitting in the worship service of your church. For Harry, it's business as usual. Let's also assume that you are the brother or sister who initiated the first two unsuccessful steps. Harry has rejected you and the others who have loved him enough to speak the truth. He will no longer discuss the matter, so you're faced with the command to "tell it to the church."

Does Jesus demand that you and the witnesses stand

up during the worship service and publicly announce Harry's sin? "Pastor, congregation, this man is living in unrepentant adultery and has sinned against God and his family by his pursuit of unbiblical divorce." Now that would liven up the service! Anyone prone to napping through the sermon would be all eyes and ears.

Is this what Jesus has in mind when he exhorts us, "tell it to the church"? Actually, the proper question to ask is, Who is the church? Who does the Lord have in mind here?

The Buck Stops at the Top

It is best to interpret the "church" in this context as the God-ordained leaders of a local body—that is, the pastor, elders, or deacons, depending on the church's form of government. The leaders are responsible to represent the congregation and to field these issues first. Much as a farmer keeps briars and nettles from the vines, the leaders are to be the first to prune and clip with disciplinary shears.

The Old Testament governmental system supports the view that the leaders represent the whole body. When God desired to speak to his people, he assembled the elders and addressed them (Ex. 3:15-16; 19:3,7; Deut. 31:28,30). The Scriptures call these assembled elders "Israel." Some scholars argue that in the apostolic church, Christ's authority was at work in the *leadership*. It would be difficult for the church to exercise any authority apart from the elders.[1]

Paul defends this view when he puts the responsibility to discipline on those "who are spiritual" (Gal. 6:1). The leaders of any church should be the first to meet such a requirement, or they shouldn't be allowed to serve at all.

Both Timothy (Titus 3:10) and Paul (2 Thess. 3:14), acting as responsible leaders, were the first to deal with a sin problem in a local church. Their example supports the contention that the leaders should be the first to handle step three.

Don't Hang Dirty Laundry in Public

Serious damage could be caused if members of the body were free to administer public discipline without the supervision of the church leaders. Other scriptural mandates would be violated, such as 1 Cor. 14, which calls for order in the worship meeting. Open announcements would not only destroy the spirit of worship but could break into a heated fight, destroying the spirit of unity.

Also, a public scene would be a bad testimony to any nonbelievers who might be present (1 Corinthians 14:23-25). A fellowship's dirty socks should never be aired in public.

Therefore, the leaders represent the church and act as shepherds, guarding its purity. If judgment must be made, it falls first to those who watch over the flock. How is this to be done?

First, Jesus understood the necessity for the increasing involvement of others to restore the brother. But to maintain decency and order, the leaders should be informed first, not the entire church. Each person who participated in step two should communicate this information either in writing or in person.

Second, the leaders are responsible to lovingly confront the wrongdoer about the accusations. The field of involvement is widened, and the church, represented by its leaders, becomes the last board of appeal. However, the church is not an appellate court or examining body; this is not a trial. Rather, the purpose for bringing the matter before the church is to involve godly men and women in strengthening the original warning and exhorting the unrepentant to return to a pure Christian walk. *The purpose is not punishment but discipline, not ridicule but restoration.*

> Punishment is designed to execute retribution for wrong doing. Discipline, on the other hand, is designed to encourage the restoration of one involved in wrong doing. Punishment is designed primarily to avenge a wrong and assert justice. Discipline is designed primarily as a corrective for the one who has failed to live according to the standards of the church and/or society.[2]

Remember, the New Testament does not allow for retribution to be disguised as discipline. God reserves retribution for himself: " 'It is mine to avenge; I will repay,' says the Lord" (Rom. 12:19).

Finally, how should the process be applied by the leaders? Jesus gave leaders a clear responsibility but without a detailed instruction book for involving the congregation. At some designated time, the fellowship needs to be involved in the discipline. Asking certain members to pray for or contact the offender by telephone or letter would be a way of broadening the family's involvement. Each situation requires a different approach, orchestrated by the leadership of the church.

Any disciplinary matter should be brought before the congregation with prayerful planning and sensitivity. If the wrongdoer acknowledges his sin at any point in the procedure, he should be forgiven and restored by the entire congregation. There is no indication that anything but sincere repentance is necessary for a full restoration.

When Step Three Fails

In the midst of Harry's rebellious life, much love was expressed toward him. The men who had faithfully tried to woo him back to Christ met privately with the elder board. Several of the elders had already heard rumors. Their first plan was to pray for Harry and to call him every other day throughout the next few weeks. After self-examination to avoid hypocrisy, each man took a day of the week and telephoned Harry's new apartment. If Harry answered, the conversation was lovingly honest. If he was not home, his answering machine recorded the gentle message and a Scripture or two. Several weeks went by before the elders also asked a selected number of Harry's Christian friends to contact him.

Over several months, the church pleaded with Harry to change his heart. During this time, his wife was being cared for and supported by the fellowship. Harry, however, had grown cold toward God as he continued in the adulterous affair and his pursuit of a divorce. It had been months since he had attended a worship service. Nothing seemed to soften him.

Treat Him as a Pagan and a Tax Collector

Jesus anticipated that a fourth step might be necessary, and he addresses it in the last half of Matthew 18:17.

> "And if he refuses to listen even to the church, treat him as you would a pagan or a tax collector."

In the event an errant brother refuses to repent, even after the prayers and exhortations of the church, a more drastic measure becomes necessary. This fourth and final step demands unusually hard love. Now he is to be treated as "a pagan or a tax collector." What exactly does Jesus mean by this?

Ancient Attitudes

To the disciples a pagan (or gentile) was a person born of another nationality and, therefore, outside the Jewish community. A pagan was an alien without any claim to God's favor; none of God's blessings belonged to him (Ezra 10:1-17; Neh. 13:1-9). A gentile in the days of Jesus was not even allowed to pass beyond the outer court of the temple without harsh penalties. Essentially, the Jews avoided them. This gives a good clue as to the attitude the church is to assume toward the rebellious brother. He is to be considered "outside" the community of believers.

When Jesus refers to a "tax collector," he has in mind a shady figure. Zacchaeus was one such weasel in the New Testament (Luke 19:2-10). Tax collectors were regarded by the average Jew as little better than robbers. Even though they were Jews, they were an offense to their Jewish heritage because they collected revenue for the pagan Roman government. Moreover, they frequently collected more than the government required. The tax collections of a particular district were leased for a fixed annual sum by the tax collector. If the collector could forcibly collect an excess above the required tax base, that amount became his. With the help of a few burly, sword-bearing Roman soldiers, a lot of profit could be made.

Tax collectors were traitors who served a pagan government at the expense of their own countrymen. They were partners with the enemy. They were regarded as apostates, outcasts, defectors from the Jewish religious life. They were looked upon as those who caused injury to God's people.

So what does Jesus mean "treat him as you would a

pagan or a tax collector"? Jesus intended the church to treat the errant brother as a Christian who has *forfeited* his rights and privileges within the local fellowship. This is what Paul did with the brother living with his stepmother at Corinth (1 Cor. 5:1-5). He told the church to remove the offender's privileges as a member of that local body.

The removal of community privileges means several things. First, the brother would no longer be considered a member of the local church. His "membership card" would be torn up, his membership terminated. As harsh as it sounds, the church would begin to view this Christian as someone outside the bride of Christ.

Next, treating him as a pagan or tax gatherer demands that he be removed from the care and support of the fellowship. The relationships that previously existed with his Christian friends are from that moment changed. He ceases to be to them anything more than an unbeliever outside the family of God. Each member of the fellowship is now bound to treat him as one belonging to the world.

Finally, he is to be treated as a nonbeliever, an unregenerate person outside the community of Christ. As any non-Christian, he would be welcome at a worship service (if his presence would not disturb those he may have hurt or cause other disruptions in the unity of the spirit). Hearing the gospel proclaimed is a privilege that every unbeliever should have. However, communion, fellowship, and meetings for support or ministry are *closed*. Since he gives no evidence of being a believer, he is to be treated as such until he repents. When the opportunity arises, we are to witness to him in order to win him back to his Savior.

As difficult as this step may be and as harsh as it may seem, the course to be pursued is confirmed by the remainder of the New Testament witnesses:

- "Keep away from them" (Rom. 16:17).
- "With such a man do not even eat" (1 Cor. 5:11).
- "Take special note of him. Do not associate with him, in order that he may feel ashamed. Yet do not regard him as an enemy, but warn him as a brother" (2 Thess. 3:14-15).

Remember, the goal is restoration above all else!

Beware of Formulas, but . . .

Every situation that demands discipline will have countless variables. Each problem will be unique, calling for a customized approach. Since Jesus knew the hearts of men, he was fully aware of the need for flexibility. In applying the principles of church discipline, always follow the four steps, but beware of rigid formulas. Below, I've outlined the basic path the New Testament gives.

Steps for the Proper Exercise of Church Discipline

1. Instruct and prepare the church body and the leadership. The church should know God's purposes for the exercise of corrective discipline (see chapter 5) and understand that it must be done in faith (Rom. 4:20). This step is preliminary to the proper exercise of discipline and should be an ongoing process.

2. Be sure the offense is "discipline worthy!" Does the offense fall outside the moral boundaries given by the New Testament? Does the sin violate Christian law, unity, love, or truth? (see chapter 10).

3. Is the sin public or private? This reveals at what level the discipline process should begin. Private sins call for step one; highly visible public sins might begin with

steps two or three if both guilt and an unrepentant attitude are obvious.

4. *Step one (Matt. 18:15).* Meet one-on-one with the offender to seek repentance and restoration.

5. *Step two (Matt. 18:16).* Widen the appeal for repentance through the involvement of other brothers as witnesses.

6. *Step three (Matt. 18:17a).* Communicate the problem and the lack of repentance to the church leaders.

7. *Step four (Matt. 18:17b).* Remove all membership responsibilities and privileges from the offender, who is to be treated as a non-Christian. This step is a formal exercise done first by the leaders of the church.

8. Notify church members in a private meeting or by confidential letter (to be destroyed) that they are not to fellowship with the offender until repentance is demonstrated.

9. Watch and pray that the offender will restore his walk with Christ and his relationship to Christ's body.

By What Power and Whose Authority?

Doing discipline correctly takes commitment. Proceeding with careful and prayerful precision requires courage and risk. But as the quiz at the beginning of the chapter reminds us (the correct answer to each question is "c"), discipline is surgery that brings ultimate healing. In fact, God's people run a greater risk when they fail to discipline (1 Cor. 11:31-32) than when they courageously choose to obey.

With such an endeavor, there needs to be a sense of confidence, an assurance that the power and authority to initiate and carry out the practice are given from heaven.

Jesus anticipated that his Bride would need just such an assurance and, in Matthew 18:18-20, he boldly gives that power and authority to the church—power and authority that every Christian should understand.

A SUMMARY OF THE PROCEDURE
FOR CORRECTIVE CHURCH DISCIPLINE
Matthew 18:15-20

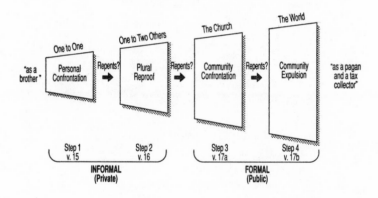

Notes

1. R. R. Williams, *Authority and the Apostolic Age* (London: Northumberland Press, 1950), 113.

2. Carl Laney, *A Guide to Church Discipline* (Minneapolis: Bethany House Publishers, 1985), 79.

By What Power and Whose Authority?

The Master understands the heart of man. He understands our motives and intentions. When he directed his church to deal with impurity, he knew there would be resistance.

Defiance. Jesus anticipated a hostile spirit from some who were under discipline. When the church begins to discipline, many unwise Christians will defiantly leave, slamming the door behind them and muttering, "The church has no right to meddle in my life; I'll go elsewhere. I'll find a church where the people are less judgmental and mind their own business." Others will walk away from all spiritual relationships, intending never to return. Either way, Jesus expected defiance from some believers whose lives were off center.

Dread. Jesus also knew that those given the heavy load of keeping the body pure would dread the thought of discipline. Jesus foresaw that some would openly express, "This matter of discipline is too risky, it's too difficult. We can't do it!" He knew the church would feel helpless, apathetic, and void of power.

In Matthew 18:18-20, the Savior deals with these two responses. In these encouraging verses, he reveals by *what power* and *whose authority* loving discipline is to be done.

"I tell you the truth, whatever you bind on earth will be bound in heaven, and whatever you loose on earth will be loosed in heaven.

"Again, I tell you that if two of you on earth agree about anything you ask for, it will be done for you by my Father in heaven. For where two or three come together in my name, there am I with them."

A Runner in the Night:
The Binding and Loosing Power of the Church

The police helicopter awakened me with a pounding rhythm. Its piercing searchlight systematically eyed every alley and driveway in the neighborhood. As I stood on the back porch watching, it was obvious they were looking for someone . . . and looking intently. At one point, the big light in the sky fell directly on me, causing me to jump back under shadow of the porch eaves and raising my heartbeat. The helicopter's presence lasted most of the night.

The next morning, the checker at the corner convenience store had the answers to all my questions. It seems a thief had been on a robbing spree, and the police took to the sky to catch him. It was impossible to escape. It didn't matter where he tried to hide or how fast he drove through the neighborhoods, the eye in the sky stayed fixed on its target all through the night. Just before daylight, he was apprehended in a local park. Some things in life are difficult to escape.

When Jesus says, "Whatever you bind on earth will be bound in heaven," he gives the church authority to either "bind or loose" any Christian under discipline in order that Kingdom affairs might properly be administered. Discipline is one thing in life that cannot be escaped. The mutinous Christian who assumes that walking away from the church's discipline will remove him from God's discipline is mistaken. When discipline is exercised on a believer, it doesn't matter where he goes—he becomes like a fugitive in the night, trying to escape the disciplinary eye of God. But the bright searchlight of heaven is never removed. Only repentance can flip the off switch.

"I Tell You the Truth . . ."

Some commentators believe that verses 18-20 are not a continuation of Jesus' teaching on discipline but are about the unrelated topics of exorcism and prayer. However, the phrase "I tell you the truth," is a familiar formula found twenty-eight times in the New Testament. In only one of these usages does the phrase introduce a new topic. This gives strong support to the view that verses 15-20 form a unit. Jesus is not introducing a new subject but continuing his teaching on church discipline. This is significant, because verses 18-20 put heavenly teeth into the practice of corrective discipline.

The phrase also suggests that great authority is to be

placed on the upcoming statements of Jesus. It is analogous to the Old Testament prophetic pronouncement, "Thus says the Lord." "I tell you the truth" expresses the authority of Jesus as a prophet and the founder of the church. It indicates that the words expressed in the "binding" and "loosing" command are from God himself, and the church is given God's authority in dealing with unrepentant sin.

The Authority for Binding and Loosing

The proverbial statement, "Whatever you bind on earth will be bound in heaven, and whatever you loose on earth will be loosed in heaven," is not difficult to understand if it is seen as another aspect of Jesus' teaching on discipline. To clarify that understanding, we need to answer three questions:

Who is to assume authority for the "binding" and "loosing" discipline?

What meaning do the unusual verbs, "will be bound and will be loosed" bring to the exercise?

What does the Son of God mean by the terms *binding* and *loosing*?

The Keys to the Kingdom

In Matthew 16, Jesus first reveals his plan to build his church. There he proclaims to Peter, "I will give you the keys of the kingdom of heaven; whatever you bind on earth will be bound in heaven, and whatever you loose on earth will be loosed in heaven" (v. 19).

Even though the reference to the "keys of the kingdom" is absent in Matthew 18:18, the concept of the keys and the authority given to the church are at the root of the power to "bind" and "loose." As I contended in chapter 3, Matthew 16 and 18 are connected, and both transfer supernatural authority to the church for discipline in Jesus' name. A proper understanding of "the keys" will answer the question, Who is to assume authority for binding and loosing?

An Old Testament illustration is found in Isaiah 22:22. In this passage, the prophet records God's commitment to Eliakim, an official in the court of Hezekiah: "I will place on his shoulder the key to the house of David; what he opens no one can shut, and what he shuts no one can open." In ancient times, a house steward carried the keys of his master's house and bore responsibility for its administration. This included the "opening" and "closing" of the residential or palace doors. The exercise of authority was associated with the possession of the house key, so the key became symbolic of authority.

In the New Testament, John records his vision of Christ having "the keys of death and Hades" (Rev. 1:18). The possession of the "keys" indicates Christ's sovereign authority over death and Hades. Also, in Revelation 3:7, Christ cites the Isaiah 22:22 passage when he refers to himself as the one "who holds the key of David. What he opens no one can shut, and what he shuts no one can open." Here again, the key is symbolic of authority.

The meaning is not foggy; the keys are synonymous with God-given authority and responsibility. In Matthew 16:18, Peter is given apostolic and administrative authority in God's kingdom program. In Matthew 18:18, Jesus switches from the singular pronoun "you" found in 16:18 to the plural "you." This grammatical change transfers to all disciples the authority Jesus first delegated to Peter "as a representative disciple."[1] This grammatical change also suggests that the authority to "bind and loose" does not rest on the apostles only; the responsibility to "bind and loose" belongs to the whole church.

To further support the argument that Jesus was not addressing the apostles only, the instructions given in verse 15, "and if your brother sins," gives the command a general thrust. Jesus did not intend discipline to be exercised only on sinning apostles. Therefore, the authority symbolized by the keys has been entrusted to the entire church, starting with the apostles and extending throughout the church age.

Tension over the Tenses: The Significance of the Verbs

The verbs *bind* and *loose* come from Christ's lips with uncommon and unexpected tenses. In the original Greek text these two verbs are problematic. Some Bible scholars read them as simple futures in tense and translate them, as the NIV does, "whatever you bind on earth *will be bound* in heaven, and whatever you loose on earth *will be loosed* in heaven." This interpretation of the verbs seems to give authority to the church to *literally* forgive human sin.

However, the best evidence argues for the very unusual usage of future perfect verbs. I know it's been too long since your last English grammar class, but this more restrictive and unexpected usage would read, "Whatever you *shall bind* on earth *shall have been bound* in heaven, and whatever you *shall loose* on earth *shall have been loosed* in heaven." Can you see the difference? Its meaning makes a world of difference. Using the future perfect tense, the verse would be best paraphrased:

> I tell you the truth, whomever you disfellowship ["bind"] from the community has already been cut off from fellowship with God, and whomever

you restore ["loose"] to fellowship with the community has already been restored to fellowship with God.

These verbs show that Jesus is not giving the church the authority to forgive sins; rather, the verbs confirm that God endorses the disciplinary actions of the church when they are handled according to divine directions. One theologian summarizes this understanding well:

> Jesus is teaching that church discipline will have heavenly sanction. But it is not as if the church must wait for God to endorse its actions; rather, whenever it enacts discipline it can be confident that God has already begun the process spiritually. Whenever it releases from discipline, forgives the sinner, and restores personal relationships, it can be confident that God has already begun the restoration spiritually (cf. John 20:23). Earthly church discipline involves the awesome certainty that corresponding heavenly discipline has already begun.[2]

Binding and Loosing?

The Lord's use of *bind* and *loose* has been subject to many different interpretations. As just mentioned, some view the terms as giving the church the authority to forgive sins. But only God has such authority! Others see it as giving the church the power to "bind and loose" demons. Both interpretations are difficult to defend, especially since the context is dealing with discipline. The best way to interpret Jesus' use of these terms is to look into contemporary Jewish culture. "Binding and loosing" have roots in rabbinical language and practice, and the disciples understood it well.

In the disciples' day, these terms were used for a rabbi's prerogative to restrict participation in the spiritual activities of the Jewish community. He could "forbid" or "permit," that is, "bind" or "loose" an errant party from involvement. Occasionally, the terms were used, in both Hebrew and Aramaic, to mean "to excommunicate or, in some instances, to restore from excommunication." Josephus, the Jewish historian, supports this usage when he records the level of spiritual authority the Jewish leaders had: "But these Pharisees . . . banished and reduced whom they pleased; they bound and loosed [men] at their pleasure."[3]

The binding and loosing in Matthew 18:18 describes the authority given to the church for both removal (step four) and restoration. It is attested in the rabbinical literature which would have been familiar to Christ and his men.

Let's put verse 18 in focus. Jesus has given the local church the authority to exercise discipline. When discipline is undertaken, heaven enters into the process and God does a supernatural work in the life of the errant brother. If the church exercises the final step in discipline, the wrongdoer is "bound." He may run—even to the far reaches of the earth—but he cannot hide. The "binding" will still be in effect.

Along with the power to "bind" comes the parallel authority to "loose" the *repentant* brother from godly discipline. When the church sees the need to discipline the errant person after attempting reconciliation, God affirms and stands behind it. The "binding and loosing" authority given to the church reminds every Christian to beware— sin and its consequences cannot be escaped.

I'm aware of how militant such a thought is, but this

is not retribution. The church is actually an arm of mercy rather than a fist of judgment. It's the church's responsibility to tell every rebellious Christian that God will not let him go! Christ gave his life for that brother, and the sovereign discipline of God cannot be escaped. The bright light of God's judgment has an endless energy source.

In one California case, a homosexual Christian was lovingly confronted by the leaders in his church, but he refused to repent. Finally, the church was forced to take the final step and regard him as a "pagan or a tax collector." He was "bound" by the church and placed under the discipline of God. The church had done all it could do. The brother silently but defiantly disappeared from the fellowship. But after five years of running he realized he could not escape the searchlight of God's discipline. The "binding" was constantly with him. After years of separation, he wrote the church about his sin and repentance:

> It is impossible for me to retrace my footsteps and right every wrong; however, I welcome the opportunity to meet and pray with any individuals who have something against me that needs resolution. I am looking and waiting for the further grace and mercy of God in this matter. What you have bound on earth has been bound in heaven, and I now know your actions were done in love for my own good and that of the body of Christ.[4]

This errant brother realized that the same authority that had "bound" him could now act upon his confession and "loose" him. The keys that Christ gave to the church can both close and open.

Although those who rebel *seem* to avoid discipline by fleeing, a spiritual eye of discipline can be placed over a

Christian by a disciplinary act from his church. Even if the brother escapes to a grass hut in the outback of Australia, he will still be "bound" by the supernatural authority Jesus gave his church. God's relentless glare is on him even if he tries to escape into the darkness of his own rebellious world.

Whether it be five or twenty-five years, the spiritual lock remains and only the church has the key. Until the errant brother repents, receives forgiveness, and returns to the place of "binding," there can be no "loosing" and ultimate healing and restoration. He is a runner in the night, spiritually handcuffed and pursued by an escort of discipline. He never gets away from the Spirit of God (Psalm 139:7).

Even though it would be ideal, the offender does not have to reunite with the fellowship and continue in that Christian community as though nothing had happened. But he must contact the leaders and express repentance and seek official forgiveness. It is important for him to return to the same door from which he exited. The Spirit of God can lead from there.

Dealing with the Defiant

Why proceed with discipline if the wrongdoer leaves the church and goes elsewhere? Hasn't the church done her duty? If the brother leaves in defiance during step three, why go on to step four? The answer is—love. Discipline is a powerful tool in the local church, and the most loving thing to do for an errant brother is to place him under discipline's "binding" authority.

Paul says in 1 Corinthians 5:5, "Hand this man over to Satan, so that the sinful nature may be destroyed and his spirit saved on the day of the Lord." The long-term spiritual good in Paul's mind should also be in the mind of the church. Public censure is an act of "binding" and the most loving thing the church can do.

In the binding and loosing responsibility, nothing is said about the errant brother's salvation. When possible, we are to share Christ and his love to encourage a return, but the church is not responsible to make judgments about the disciplined brother's eternal destiny; only God is able to save. The church is given the mandate of protecting the offender's relationship with Christ and the church, not of making eternal judgments about salvation.

Finally, if the errant brother takes refuge in another church, should that church be notified? Jesus doesn't address this point, but it is a practical problem that will likely surface. The discipline of "binding" will follow the offender wherever he goes. The church has done all it can; it should not have the spirit of a "bounty hunter." However, as a pastor, I want to know if a new participant in our fellowship is under some form of discipline. The same impurity that caused the discipline may be brought into my fellowship and contaminate a new group of God's people. Also, if the new fellowship knew of the discipline, it could assist in the offender's restoration and return to spiritual health.

Notifying other churches caused the Collinsville Church of Christ in Tulsa, Oklahoma, to lose a four-day jury trial and $390,000.[5] The jury interpreted the contacting of sister churches in the city as "harassment." In this case, the contact was unwise since the unrepentant offender had not visited any other churches; cooperative discipline was unnecessary. Since the church can make serious mistakes in this area, a few guidelines might be helpful.

First, another fellowship should not be contacted

unless there is substantial evidence that the offender has become a regular participant in that fellowship. Second, the pastor of the "binding" fellowship should contact the pastor of the new church to explore his (and the church's) position on discipline and his interest in knowing about the spiritual condition of one of his new participants. In many cases, tragically, the leadership will have no interest in learning about the new visitor. At no time should a mass mailing be sent to stop the offender from finding another fellowship. That would be harassment and, possibly, even slander. Be assured that God follows the steps of his own and is concerned with the offender's spiritual state. We are to be as wise as serpents but gentle as doves.

Jesus foresaw one final issue: What about those who dread the responsibility to exercise discipline? In timidity and fear, many of God's people feel powerless to participate in such an exercise. Because of this, apathy over sin in our churches is rampant today. Is there any help for the weak-kneed?

Divine Presence in Dreadful Situations

Matthew 18:18 gives the promise of heavenly authority for church discipline and verses 19-20 give the promise of Christ's counsel and direction in the heat of the battle:

> "Again, I tell you that if two of you on earth agree about anything you ask for, it will be done for you by my Father in heaven. For where two or three come together in my name, there am I with them."

At times, our churches seem apathetic and void of spiritual clout. This is true, in part, because the body of Christ has overlooked two of the most encouraging passages in the Bible. The church's fear should be calmed when we realize how active a role Jesus takes in the discipline process. The presence of the risen Christ will be in the very midst of every struggle to lovingly correct a brother.

Verses 19-20 are typically understood as an encouragement for Christians to gather together and pray. Certainly, prayer pleases God and is an essential part of every believer's growth; however, these verses are not primarily a promise concerning prayer. This passage is about loving discipline. Jesus promises his presence whenever the church gathers to exercise discipline. Now that is a comfort.

How can we be sure verses 19-20 are a continuation of Jesus' teachings on discipline and not about prayer or the value of small-group meetings? First, Jesus says the church binds "on earth" in verse 18 and she prays "on earth" in verse 19. There is a logical connection between praying and the discipline of "binding." Second, verse 19 begins with "again," making a clear connection between it and verse 18. Finally, the word "anything" in verse 19 can carry the specific sense of "judicial matters" or weighty issues of the law. Jesus is not calling the Christian to lift up in prayer "anything" or "any complication of life" that might need prayer, but to pray over the outcome of the practice of discipline. The formal removal of a believer from the fellowship is a "judicial matter" worthy of prayer. Jesus' teaching on discipline extends from verse 15 through verse 20.

Agreement on the Earth

Jesus' conditional statement in verse 19—"if two of you on earth agree about anything you ask for"—suggests that believers who come together over a ruptured disciplinary situation should have reached agreement about the need for discipline and its proper exercise. *Agree* is the key word, and this basic principle should not be overlooked: harmony is essential for proper discipline to be carried out. For God to respond positively to their prayers, the leaders need to be in agreement. They need to come alongside each other and find agreement through biblical research, prayer, and discussion. Jesus' mention of the number of participants ("two or three, v. 20") reflects back to verse 16, where he cites the need for agreement among those who initiate step two as witnesses.

Jesus is encouraging the fellowship to come together to pray about the discipline process he outlined in verses 15-18. He is teaching that discipline must be guarded and directed by prayer in order to maintain a proper spirit of humility and godly concern for the offender. In order to make decisions that are authored by God, we must have prayer and unity.

Christ in the Midst

Jesus concludes his teaching with a divine promise: He will actively participate with those involved in the prayerful process. When the process begins and a meeting is called for prayer and God's guidance, Jesus comes to the meeting! The Christian community's decision is coordinated with heaven's action, because Christ is present in the assembly. What a powerful promise!

Verse 20 stands as Christ's personal encouragement to every board or committee that dreads the call of purity but must face it with courage. The Spirit of Jesus will be present in the decision-making process, guiding and encouraging each member and directing the outcome.

As a pastor, I have experienced this wonderful promise. As our board has met to prayerfully consider steps of love in a member's life, we have felt the guiding presence of our Savior. His presence gives us calmness and an unusual measure of love and compassion. We have avoided many mistakes because he has led us. He has kept his promise . . . he has been there!

Christ cares about the purity of his church (Rev. 3:19), and he promises his presence in the midst of the difficult process of discipline. Whether it be discipline of a pastor who is abusing his authority or of a slanderer whose tongue has become a "fire starter" in your church, Christ will be in the midst of the cooperative effort to exercise "tough love" to all involved. The church cannot afford to be without Christ in such difficult times.

The phrase "in my name" commits the very authority of Christ to the exercise. It denies that the discipline was the act of one person or a vigilante act of the whole church. It means that the church has the divine right to act as the disciplinary agent of the Lord. Sometimes a church has to have its spiritual mettle tested through a few "truth struggles." What a comfort it is to have the Lord actively in our presence!

Feeling the Power and Authority

Do you remember Harry from the previous chapter? In his case, all four steps were lovingly followed. I know, because he was a member of my church. Yes, he was defiant. Yes, we dreaded the process. Yes, we felt the Savior's presence and miraculous assistance. Yes, God's light of scrutiny is presently on him. Three days after the church prayed that God would "bind" Harry and return him to Christ, to his family, and to his church, he was mysteriously and painfully stricken with an illness. The doctor warned him it could have been fatal. During this time, the

Internal Revenue Service contacted him to pursue an audit. His behavior has become unreasonable and frantic, and his job is in constant jeopardy. Harry is feeling the scrutiny of God's love. He is feeling the heat from the Light of the world. As his Savior pursues him, we're prayerfully waiting for Harry to come home.

Meet the Frightening Five

Since the Reformation, there has been a steady decline in the practice of discipline in the Christian community. Even though God's people are promised divine presence during the struggle, the church still avoids the practice. In the next chapter, I consider five reasons the church is afraid to exercise any authority over the lives of God's people. One reason is that many churches today are not aware of what specific sins call for discipline. What sins are "discipline worthy"?

Notes

1. Robert H. Gundry, *Matthew: A Commentary on His Literary and Theological Art* (Grand Rapids, Mich.: Wm. B. Eerdmans Publishing Co., 1982), 369.

2. *Evangelical Dictionary of Theology*, s.v. "Keys of the Kingdom."

3. Josephus, *Jewish Wars* 1.5.2.

4. Mark R. Littleton, "Church Discipline: A Remedy to What Ails the Body," *Christianity Today*, 8 May 1981, 33.

5. Interview with Elder Ted Moody, *The Christian Chronicle*, April 1984, 1.

CHAPTER TEN

What Sins Demand Our Attention?

The First Church of Newburg was enthusiastic about its new pastor, Pete Donovan, a handsome, single man in his midthirties. Over the four years he served, they began to refer to him as the "knight on a white horse." Donovan was a man with "personal charisma: the winning smile; the sincere, intense eye contact; the warm, caring hug."[1] However, events soon happened that shook the foundation of the church and tested its integrity.

In her book, *Is Nothing Sacred?* Marie Fortune writes about the victims of Peter Donovan, and how the church feared confronting his sin and its aftershock:

> Formal complaints of professional misconduct by the pastor of the First Church of Newburg were brought by six women. The charges

included sexual contact with counselees and employees, misuse of his pastoral office to coerce or manipulate parishioners, verbal threats to intimidate people who might report his activities, and the use of physical force to engage in sexual intercourse. There was evidence that as many as forty-five church members may have been victims of Peter Donovan.[2]

But once the complaints were lodged, neither the pastor nor the church leadership were prepared or willing to respond. First Church tried to protect itself by preventing disclosure of the misconduct and by denigrating the women who had the courage to tell the dark secrets.

But protecting unethical individuals from the consequences of their unprofessional conduct ultimately undermines the credibility of the entire institution. As a result, all the designated leaders become implicitly untrustworthy and the institution becomes a sham. Eventually, the institution may realize that its interests are in fact not served by avoidance. . . . The institution has the power and responsibility to protect the people it is called to serve, thereby safeguarding its own credibility. Once it accepts this responsibility, it has the capacity to name the evil in its midst and to act justly in order to rectify harm done. . . .

The church has a choice when faced with such occurrences: It can turn a deaf ear, or it can heed the call of its own theology.[3]

After months of struggle, Donovan voluntarily resigned on the condition that there be no public disclosure. The First Church of Newburg was a church afraid of discipline.

There are at least five reasons the prospect of discipline frightens most Christians, including our church leaders. Let's examine each of those reasons and how to overcome them.

Overcoming the Frightening Five

First, discipline is difficult to consider because many churches do not know where to begin. This is especially true of churches that have never made any attempt to restrain open sin. The larger the fellowship, the more irregularities there will be. At times, unaddressed sin can be so prevalent that the leaders are at a loss to know how or where to begin. If they make an attempt, they come under criticism for being unfair and inconsistent with past offenders who were not approached.

Nevertheless, a body that seeks the power of Christ's presence needs to take the risk and begin. God will honor the church's obedience. Even though some churches have allowed offenses to go unchecked, when discipline does begin and the dust settles, a purer church will emerge. The bride of Christ will return to holy living and acquire a much-needed reputation for practicing what it preaches.

Second, it's frightening to confront sin when it might cause major disruptions in the church. The hard feelings and damaged relationships can cause members to recoil from one another in bitterness and criticism. When people become upset and spin out of the church, confusion and misunderstandings cut like a knife.

But if handled properly, discipline can be an act of love and caring that is attractive to a hurting world, where love is so often phony. Discipline properly administered can remove spiritual blindness and confusion; even more significantly, it pleases God.

Third, it's frightening to consider how easily discipline could become abusive and destructive. Mishandled authority is always dangerous, as church history reveals. Because the church at times has been guilty of abuse, discipline should be done with great care, love, and much prayer. Holding restoration as the highest aim for the offender's life keeps the process a healthy act of love and not a flexing of spiritual muscle.

Fourth, it's frightening to look around at the larger body of Christ and notice the glaring lack of role models to emulate. Within the local church there seem to be few believers who admonish other Christians when they observe them walking dangerously close to the faultline. Likewise, there is a void of models to follow among the nation's Christian leadership. To whom do we look for skill and courage? What national spiritual figure stands publicly for healing discipline? The church today must look to the life of Christ as our model, which is actually much better than following after fallible men.

Fifth, and probably of greatest consequence, few are clear on what sins should be confronted. Few church leaders are able to articulate what sins demand disciplinary attention. The boundaries that alert us to the need for discipline are hazy.

What Sins Wave the Red Flag?

Which of these actions do you consider worthy of disciplinary intervention?

- The prominent doctor who teaches Sunday school in the three-year-old class and performs abortions on Monday?

- The businessman who gives generously to the church but operates a phony mail-order cosmetics business?

- The husband and father who is so slothful that he is gainfully employed only one day a week and his front yard looks like the city dump?

- The middle-aged man or woman who has wrestled from youth with the habit of smoking?

- The couple who has filed for divorce?

- The abusive father?

- The college junior who has a reputation for being a drinking, swearing, and carousing party animal?

- The office receptionist who is a compulsive eater and seems to gain more weight from Sunday to Sunday?

Few would disagree that murder and adultery are outside the boundaries of acceptable behavior, but what about a fellow believer who is a glutton or an abusive employer? What sins wave the red flag? When Jesus says to begin the discipline process "if your brother sins against you" (Matt. 18:15), does he mean *any* and *all* sin? How narrow or broad are the sin boundaries put forth by the New Testament? Fortunately, the answer can remove much of the fear of practicing discipline.

A History of Listing

The question, "What sins call for discipline?" has been debated throughout church history. In the Reformation period, Martin Luther threatened to excommunicate a brother who intended to sell a house he had purchased for 30 guilders to a willing buyer for a whopping 400 guilders. Luther suggested 150 guilders and labeled the unwilling offender as one in need of discipline for unbridled greed.[4]

In early American life, the Puritans, under Cotton Mather, disciplined for a broad range of sins such as, "swearing, cursing, sabbath-breaking, drunkenness, fighting, defamation, fornication, unchastity, cheating, stealing, idleness, lying, and 'such Heresies as manifestly overturn the Foundations of the *Christian Religion* and of all PIETY.' "[5]

Other Puritan lists included matters of political and social evil, slaveholding, participation in the magistracy, participation in the military and in war, child labor, excessive profits, collaboration with oppressive governments, usury, racial discrimination, smuggling, cockfighting, bull-baiting, tax evasion, and rioting.[6] There doesn't seem to be anything the Puritans wouldn't discipline!

These lists should not surprise us since it has been the practice of the body of Christ to compile countless legalistic lists.

Numerous writers in the history of Christianity have attempted to compile a catalog of sins that offers a reliable guide for initiating church discipline. Some have even sought to establish a graduated scale of sins that rather automatically triggers the appropriate response from the church—perhaps from mild admonition through public censure to full excommunication. When a given act is committed, it needs only to be classified in order for church machinery, set for the proper cycle, to be set in motion.[7]

Legalists and Lists

Of course a list, in itself useful enough, can become a rulebook that all too quickly replaces the Word and the Spirit of God. Devastating legalistic consequences result. It creates blind spots and preoccupation with some sins while others go unattended. "When seventy-five percent of a church's list of excommunications has to do with clothes, there is something woefully wrong."[8] Cataloging sins can lead to inflexible and legalistic measures that are harsh and do irrevocable damage.

The worst possibility is that these codes of conduct can confirm sinners in a works-righteousness attitude that undermines the very purpose of church discipline—to bring men and women to manifest in their lives restoration of faith. So, while categorizing sins may be somewhat helpful, we must guard against the tendency to assign degrees of value to certain behaviors while mandating penalties for the failure to meet required standards. This action could calcify the transgressor's situation and weaken the biblical purpose of loving restoration. Face it, lists can lead to dangerous legalism. Even though there is danger, this does not negate our responsibility to answer the question, "Which sins?"

The New Testament describes sins that might be labeled as categories for discipline. In addition, six passages in the New Testament illustrate the two levels of discipline that were exercised: 1) complete expulsion from the community (1 Cor. 5:5; 2 Cor. 2:5-11; Titus 3:10; Matt. 18:17) and 2) temporary shunning within the community (1 Cor. 5:11, 2 Thess. 3:14-15). To find an answer to the question, "Which sins should we discipline?" we need to start with these New Testament teachings.

Jesus Was Not a List Maker

Although no one spoke more openly against wrong than Jesus, he never gives a list of sins that call for discipline. He does, however, speak to a much more significant problem:

> "You have heard that it was said to the people long ago, 'Do not murder, and anyone who murders will be subject to judgment.' But I tell you that anyone who is angry with his brother will be subject to judgment" (Matt. 5:21-22).

To you and me, murder is worse than an outburst of anger; these two sins do not have the same horror quotient. But Jesus does not agree! He links these two sins together to demonstrate that *all* sin belongs not to the sphere of outward conduct but to that of *inner attitude*. The law condemned adultery, but Jesus condemned both adultery and lust. Christ emphasized the inner character that underlies outward conduct. He was concerned foremost with the origin of sin and not with the form in which it manifests itself. No wonder Jesus wasn't a list maker.

In Mark 7:20-23, Jesus does give a list of sins. However, as with Matthew's account, the emphasis is not on the sins themselves but upon the origin of evil—the heart of man:

> "What comes out of a man is what makes him 'unclean'. For from within, out of men's hearts, come evil thoughts, sexual immorality, theft, murder, adultery, greed, malice, deceit, lewdness, envy, slander, arrogance and folly. All these evils come from inside and make a man 'unclean.' "

Jesus is demanding inner purity. To him, all sin is

172

discipline worthy, and discipline should have its beginning in the heart. The only boundaries put forth by Jesus are those he desired to put around men's hearts.

But should the fellowship participate in heart examinations? You and I cannot see into the inner being of another. Only God can see the hearts of men, and men can know only themselves. Since we cannot judge the hearts of others, we must judge the *symptoms*, the sins that surface. A search of the rest of the New Testament reveals the sins that need attention.

When to Deal with Sin

A summary of all the New Testament Scriptures on sin points to four watershed categories rather than a large, specific list of sins. These categories embrace both the spirit (the inner man) and the law (the actions); they deal with sin as it relates to Christian love, unity, law, and truth.

Private and Personal Offenses that Violate Christian Love

To discern if an action is worthy of confrontation, we need to ask, Does that deed violate basic Christian love? The responsibility every Christian has to "love your neighbor as yourself" is high on Jesus' list of what is essential (Matt. 22:39). This commandment is to be protected and upheld in the body (Gal. 5:13; 1 Pet. 4:8; 1 John 4:7). When it is disregarded, the refusal to repent and be reconciled results in a continued breach of Christian love.

The rampant increase in divorce today has affected the kingdom of Christ. Thousands of believers file for separation and divorce every year. In the past, I believed that since divorce was not on any New Testament list of "discipline-worthy sins," I would leave it alone when its ugly head surfaced in our fellowship. Even though the Scriptures say that God hates divorce, I would sigh, hurt for the couple, and walk away. But divorce is a major violation of Christian love and offends the heart of God. No pastor could deny that it also frequently brings other disturbances into the fellowship.

At the root of every divorce is some manner of sin. It may be that years of stubbornness and unkindness have led to a root of bitterness (Heb. 12:15). Perhaps moral unfaithfulness has eroded the marriage. Even though the causes could be many and some out of the reach of formal church discipline, the law of love demands that the church at least initiate step one and contact the couple. The fellowship needs to make some effort to express love and concern and, if possible, attempt to reconcile the split.

How many families would be saved from lifelong heartache if the church would evaluate aggravated and unrepentant sin against the standard of love? Whether it be divorce, child abuse, wife beating, malicious personal rejection, or a basketful of other possibilities, all violations of the law of love are discipline worthy. Once again, the discipline may be as simple as a loving contact or as difficult as "binding" action.

Divisiveness and Factions that Destroy Christian Unity

The second category has to do with keeping peace and harmony in the fellowship. To know if a deed is worthy of discipline ask, Is this action tearing a seam in the unity of the church?

Peace and unity in the local body are essential. In Romans 16:17, Paul urges us "to watch out for those who cause divisions and put obstacles in your way that are contrary to the teaching you have learned. Keep away from them." In Galatians 5:20, he commands that the fellowship reject the deeds of the flesh such as "selfish ambition, dissensions, factions and envy." In 1 Corinthians 5:11, he exhorts the church to avoid association with a "slanderer." Likewise, John purposed to discipline even a disruptive church leader (3 John 9-10). Those who destroy peace and unity must be watched, rebuked, and, if necessary, removed.

When an associate pastor begins to lead a splinter group into his own thinking on theology or polity, he is causing a division and pulling apart the unity. Another leader needs to lovingly address his intentions. If the senior pastor begins to teach a doctrine that is contrary to the beliefs of the church and factions begin to arise, he should be approached by a close friend or a board member before the church suffers a destructive split. If a charter member has become bitter over a past hurt or disagreement with the leadership, his critical attitude will poison the entire fellowship. This is a violation of the unity of the church and should be handled in love. Proverbs 6:19 warns God's people that he hates "a man who stirs up dissension among brothers."

Unity is a precious commodity in the church today. Guard it!

Moral Deviations that Break
Biblical Commandments/Standards

Of the four categories of sin, *breaking the laws of God* is the easiest to observe and receives the lion's share of attention.

The Scriptures are filled with black and white commandments against breaking specific moral laws. It is a moral sin to commit adultery, fornication, or homosexual acts. It is a sin to lie, steal, or covet. If we want to know if an action is worthy of confrontation, ask, Does this act violate any commandment stated in Scripture?

Christian law is violated by those who insist on living unrepentant, scandalous lives. First Corinthians 5:11 asserts that believers should not keep company with a brother who is a fornicator or a drunkard. These acts break the moral code. Ephesians 5:11 teaches, "have nothing to do with the fruitless deeds of darkness, but rather expose them." Second Thessalonians 3:6 commands, "keep away from every brother who is idle and does not live according to the teaching you received from us." The law of proper Christian conduct is not to go unnoticed in the church.

Teaching of False Doctrines that Reject Essential Christian Truth

Biblical truth is under constant bombardment, yet few Christians would consider taking disciplinary action against anyone's beliefs or teachings. However, when false teaching is being injected into the local church, it *must* be addressed—with haste!

Paul instructs Titus that a church elder must "hold firmly to the trustworthy message as it has been taught, so that he can encourage others by sound doctrine and refute those who oppose it" (Titus 1:9). Paul adds a couple of chapters later: "Warn a divisive [heretical] person once, and then warn him a second time. After that, have nothing to do with him" (3:10). Many other New Testament passages speak about guarding the truth (1 Tim. 6:3-5; 2 John 7-11).

Applying these principles does *not* mean that

Christians should be censured for failing to understand and receive every doctrine revealed in the Bible. All Christians are learning and growing. Rather, this warning refers to those who knowingly reject those doctrines the church considers fundamental to the faith.

For pastors and elders, the standard is more rigid since they are responsible to teach and defend "the whole will of God" (Acts 20:27). They are responsible to maintain the essential doctrines (especially as embodied in their church's creed), and are liable to be disciplined if they fail to do so (1 Tim. 3:2,9; Titus 1:9; James 3:1).

The New Testament establishes a code of purity that demands that all *unrepentant* and *visible* transgressions be disciplined. Jesus desires self-discipline from his followers, but when self-discipline fails, the Christian community is responsible to participate in the therapy.

Handling Lists from the Future

The New Testament's sin boundaries are firm but flexible. Unmovable, rigid lists fall short because they deny each generation the responsibility of rethinking the unique transgressions of that era. The church will always discipline unrepentant adultery or murder, but if our lists are rigid, then sins yet uncommon to man would be easily overlooked.

I hope it doesn't shock you to learn that the sin potential of mankind has not yet been exhausted. Some manifestations of moral transgressions are not yet known. Scientific and medical changes in the twentieth century are a case in point. How should the church handle some of the ethical issues raised by biogenetics? Even though sexual sins are a clear violation of the laws of God, what about some of the ramifications of the AIDS epidemic? Should the church exercise punitive measures on one who has transmitted the disease? How would discipline be applied in a case where a member rejects another because of the disease? In a sense, these are old sins, but they're coming at our generation in new packaging.

The televangelist and his impact on the commitment of church members illustrates another area unrelated to the ancient church. Drug abuse, euthanasia, and abortion should also be listed. Even though some are variations of age-old sins, they can pose new dilemmas to the contemporary church that limits itself with a strict code or list of "discipline-worthy" sins.

The church of the future may have a broader and more complicated struggle with sin's many new faces. Without pliable disciplinary boundaries, Christ's bride cannot remain a covenant community, separate from the world. Instead she may become a captive of the culture. Rather than adopting the standards of the world, the church *must* return to the business of morality.

Also, in each of these four arenas, both the act of sin and the spirit of sin are considered. These classifications address a person's attitude toward God, not simply his actions. Remember, Jesus taught that sins of attitude are just as deadly as sins of action.

In all this, the church must not forget the great need for the participation of the Holy Spirit. "The work of discipline must be a spiritual work, first and foremost. It must move beyond rational ethics or the calculation of strategy and be borne along by something which gives it life."[9]

The Greatest Sin of All

There is one offense that ranks above all others, one sin that violates all four categories—an unrepentant heart.

There is always only one sin that excludes from the fellowship of God's people, and that is not the specific sin that first evokes our concern. It is rather the sinning brother's unwillingness to "hear" the pleas and admonitions of his brethren, the sin of persisting on the sinful course and of refusing to come to repentance.[10]

What about a Christian who is repentant but continues to struggle with a certain sin? Frequently a believer will repeat an offense. He wrestles within and exerts a great deal of energy to overcome the problem. He is usually repentant and filled with regret. He needs a place where every type of hurt and injury can find a bandage. The church must be that place where continuous prayer support and balanced biblical teaching and counseling and readily available. If our goal is restoration and reconciliation, a quick fix mentality will only frustrate everyone. We are all in this together . . . and if necessary for the long run. The repentant Christian who struggles with recurring sin is to be forgiven, loved, and nurtured as often as needed (Matt. 18:22).

Be sure of this, once the practice of purity becomes reality in the fellowship, the impact on unrepentant sin will be significant. Tragically, the church today has almost altogether abandoned this mandate.

A Summary of the Sins that Warrant Corrective Church Discipline

All unrepentant sin is subject to corrective discipline. The scriptural emphasis is placed on those sins that violate the purity of the Christian community. The sins that warrant church discipline in the community context are:

1. Private and personal offenses that violate Christian love.

- "If your brother sins against you" (Matt. 18:15; 5:23-24)

- Reject "discord, jealousy, fits of rage" (Gal. 5:20)

2. Divisions and factions which destroy Christian unity.

   - "Watch out for those who cause divisions" (Rom. 16:17)

   - "Warn a divisive person" (Titus 3:10)

   - "You must not associate with anyone who calls himself a brother but is . . . a slanderer" (1 Cor. 5:11)

3. Moral and ethical deviations which break Christian law.

   - "You must not associate with anyone who calls himself a brother but is sexually immoral or greedy . . . a drunkard or a swindler" (1 Cor. 5:11)

   - "We command you to keep away from every brother who is idle" (2 Thess. 3:6)

   - Reject "impurity and debauchery" (Gal. 5:19)

   - "Have nothing to do with the fruitless deeds of darkness, but rather expose them" (Eph. 5:11)

4. Teaching of false doctrines which reject essential Christian truth.

   - "Encourage others by sound doctrine and refute those who oppose it" (Titus 1:9)

   - "Contend for the faith . . . for certain men

whose condemnation was written about long ago have secretly slipped in among you" (Jude 3-4)

- "You must not associate with anyone who calls himself a brother but is . . . an idolater" (1 Cor. 5:11).

Soiled Shepherds?

But what about a fallen pastor? Should he be treated with the same consideration, or does the New Testament call for a different standard of treatment? What should be done to protect our shepherds who stand on the faultline? Should a pastor be allowed back into the ministry after a public fall? In the next section, we will focus on the problem of fallen Christian leaders and how to help your shepherd stand firm along the ever-shifting faultline.

Notes

1. Marie M. Fortune, *Is Nothing Sacred? When Sex Invades the Pastoral Relationship* (San Francisco: Harper and Row, 1989), 3.

2. Ibid., xiii.

3. Ibid., ix, xviii.

4. Ruth Gotze, *Wie Luther Kirchenzucht Ubte* (Gottingen: Vanderhoeck & Ruprecht, 1958), 110.

5. Emil Oberholzer, "Saints in Sin: A Study of the Disciplinary Action of the Congregational Churches of Massachusetts in the Colonial and Early National Periods" (Ph.D. diss., Columbia University, 1954), 31.

6. Carl D. Bangs, "The Search for the Marks of a

Disciplined Church," *Register*, January 1980, 15.

7. Marvin L. Jescke, "Toward an Evangelical Conception of Corrective Church Discipline" (Ph.D. diss. Northwestern University, 1965), 68.

8. Ibid., 76.

9. Bangs, "Marks of a Disciplined Church," 20.

10. H. J. A. Bouman, "Biblical Presuppositions for Church Discipline," *Concordia Theological Monthly* 30 (February 1959): 515.

PART FIVE

Administering First Aid to the Fallen Leader

CHAPTER ELEVEN

Faultproofing Your Shepherd: How to Keep Your Shepherd from Falling

On a comfortable May afternoon during my last week of seminary, my favorite professor shared a delightful story. As a young seminary student, he had been invited to preach in a small country church. That Sunday morning he delivered, in one twenty-minute sermon, all the biblical truth he knew. "Nothing feels better than delivering God's Word to receptive people!" he thought to himself.

When the morning worship was over and the "back slapping" complete, a small gentleman responsible for providing this city preacher's lunch introduced himself. The country gentleman's home was comfortable, and lunch was quite a spread (complete with homemade jam).

Afterward, it was time to show the young preacher the fruits of years of farming. Actually, this farmer was a sheep rancher, and a successful one at that. The two walked out to the pasture and leaned over the fence, chewing on Johnson grass for a few moments. Then the rancher, surveying his flock, said to this young would-be shepherd of God's flock, "Call the sheep over to us."

The challenge was taken, and with enthusiasm the student yelled, "Sheep, sheep, here sheepees." When you know nothing about shepherding, you assume you call sheep like you would pigs. To his surprise, nothing happened. With a little embarrassment, he made another attempt—he bleated. Finally, in frustration, windmilling his arm, he called out again. The unhurried woollies kept their heads down, passively chewing. Not even one looked up.

After an embarrassing silence, the rancher called his sheep, using similar words. At the sound of his voice, the sheep raised their heads and began to graze toward the two. It was the voice of the shepherd that motivated the sheep. Sheep know their shepherd's voice.

The same is true in the spiritual kingdom. Jesus, the Chief Shepherd, declared, "[the shepherd's] sheep follow him because they know his voice" (John 10:4). A shepherd has a big responsibility to care for his sheep, because often they will follow his leading—anywhere.

The Responsibility of the Flock

These days sheep have a responsibility not only to know and follow the voice of their earthly shepherd, but also to be a *shepherd watcher*. Matthew 7:15 warns God's sheep to be well trained in the art of shepherd watching, because some shepherds are wolves in disguise. Though most shepherds are trustworthy, some are not. Since predators can be found even in the pulpit, every sheep should have a good grasp of what a genuine shepherd looks and acts like. Every Christian should have an understanding of the character requirements for a church leader.

This chapter could be called Shepherd Watching 101. In this course, we will learn the character requirements of a genuine shepherd, what signs to look for in the life of a struggling shepherd, and how to keep your shepherd from causing aftershock.

Shepherd Watching 101

The leaders of every flock need to meet certain requirements. At the outset, a shepherd is seen in three possible roles: *pastor, elder,* and *overseer* (1 Tim. 3:1-13). The responsibilities and requirements for all three offices are virtually the same, though the terms emphasize different aspects of the shepherd's role. The designation *overseer* emphasizes the responsibility of spiritual oversight (Acts 20:17-28), *elder* stresses the spiritual maturity and dignity that service in such a position requires, and *pastor* emphasizes the shepherding of spiritual flocks (Eph. 4:11; Acts 20:28; 1 Pet. 5:2).

The Character Requirements for a Shepherd
(1 Tim. 3:1-7)

In the first century, being a Christian leader could mean severe persecution. A man aspiring to fill the office of pastor or overseer might find himself without a job, a family, or even a head! This possibility of hardship explains why Timothy needed to be encouraged by Paul to let all men who desired to become leaders know that, "if anyone sets his heart on being an overseer, he desires a noble task" (1 Tim. 3:1). But the job demanded proven character, and Paul describes those character requirements in the verses that follow.

Above Reproach (vv. 2-3)

Now the overseer must be above reproach . . .

The pastor is called an overseer because he is given the sacred trust of overseeing the souls of the sheep in his flock. With this high calling comes a corresponding demand for high character. "Since an overseer is entrusted with God's work, he must be blameless" (Titus 1:7). But what does a blameless shepherd look like?

Paul's definition of "blameless or above reproach" is given in 1 Timothy 3:2-7. It's a probing list. To be a pastor who is above reproach, a man must be:

the husband of but one wife, temperate, self-controlled, respectable, hospitable, able to teach . . . (v. 2).

Each of these needs a brief explanation.

To be "the husband of one wife" means the pastor must have been successful at the privileges and the challenges of living with only one woman. Being "temperate" implies a sober attitude and sound-minded lifestyle. He is serious about spiritual matters. After all, the soul of a person has eternal value; it must not be treated frivolously. A pastor must exhibit "self-control" in every area of life. He is to be calm. He should show good behavior and "respectability" in his dealings both inside and outside the church. To be "hospitable" is to see his home as a ministry base of operations. He is to be approachable and caring. Finally, he must know the Word of God well enough, and love it deeply enough, to "teach" it with at least average communication skills.

This shepherd is above reproach!

Next Paul warns God's sheep that a man worthy of

pastoring a flock must not be addicted to any of the four common vices of men:

> not given to drunkenness, not violent but gentle, not quarrelsome, not a lover of money (v. 3).

First, the apostle mentions "drunkenness" to emphasize that a genuine shepherd cannot have any physical addictions. An attachment to drugs and alcohol is out! The sheep should never find their shepherd out buying illegal drugs or carousing with the boys. He is to be "not violent but gentle"; he is not to be a brawler or fistfighter. Rather than exploiting anyone with physical force, he is to show gentleness and mercy. Sheep should never hear their pastor say, "If I could get my hands on that guy, I'd beat the life out of him." He must thrive on peace, not on conflict and "quarrels." When conflicts arise, he will not see it as a threat to his power. Finally, a lover of money is a person with a "me-first" attitude. A pastor's life should exhibit a love for people, not money.

A shepherd who participates in these activities is *not* above reproach!

Inside, Outside, and Around the World (vv. 4-7)

Finally, Paul spreads the requirements beyond the shepherd's character to include the nitty-gritty of his relationships with his family, church, community, and world:

> He must manage his own family well and see that his children obey him with proper respect. (If anyone does not know how to manage his own family, how can he take care of God's church?) He must not be a recent convert, or he may become conceited and fall under the same judgment as the devil. He must also have a

good reputation with outsiders, so that he will not fall into disgrace and into the devil's trap (vv. 4-7).

The pastor must be with his family enough to accept and discharge his responsibilities as husband and father. He must be a good manager in his own household. Pastors can easily place ministry before family. Eating meals together and spending evenings at home is basic to good fatherhood. As for the church, a qualified shepherd must have been in the faith long enough to have some experience and seasoning. Finally, the community should speak well of him.

Such a man is qualified to lead.

You may have noticed that Paul did not say a shepherd had to be perfect! He doesn't need to glow in the dark, feel good all the time, or ride a white horse. Intestinal viruses will strike him; he will experience frustrations, disappointments, and make mistakes. He possesses feet of clay like any human, but his life will be characterized by these basic qualifications.

Signs of a Staggering Shepherd

In his excellent article, "Why Do Ministers Fall?" Richard Dobbins lists three pressures that cause today's shepherds to stumble.[1] First, like all of us, a pastor lives in a sexually over-stimulated society that gnaws at his spirit. He is not immune to its influence. Second, the rapid rate of social change and the pace of modern life put unusual stress on people and on those ministering to them. The more God's people suffer, the harder the shepherd works at healing them. Finally, the minister is always vulnerable to the temptation to confuse "work for God" with "walk with God." These daily pressures can have an eroding effect on the strength and stamina of your pastor.

In light of his character requirements and the daily job pressure, here are a few of the signs of a staggering shepherd that every sheep should know. The two areas of concern are *character* and *ministry*.

Cracks in the Shepherd's Character

Attitude Cracks. Since a pastor is to be a servant-leader, one of the first signs of trouble is usually in the area of servanthood. If arrogance begins to show, he may be seeing his role more as a ruler than as a servant-leader. An attitude of "lording it over" the flock (1 Pet. 5:3) indicates that submissiveness to other church authorities is lacking. Manipulation of people and programs is always a danger sign. Lack of willingness to be accountable to others is also a warning. Throughout the Bible, these attitude cracks are indicators of a rebellious spirit (Jer. 23:10; Jude 6; 2 Pet. 2:10). Watch out for them.

Motivational Cracks. The second sign to watch for is a shift in a pastor's motivation for ministering. The call to be a soul-watcher can easily take a back seat to other motivations for ministry—such as money! I have met pastors who expressed disappointment and anger at salary adjustment time. They were so financially oriented they were never satisfied. If the shepherd's focus is on making more and getting further ahead, something is wrong. The love of money is a sign of cracked motivation in any shepherd's life (2 Pet. 2:15; Jude 12). A false shepherd loves money more than he loves his sheep. Beware!

Morality Cracks. Moral sins are usually the most observable. When they are finally exposed, they erupt like a volcano! The sin nature inside every shepherd can lead him into immorality, pride, and other selfish lusts (Jer. 23:14;

2 Pet. 2:10). When a shepherd begins to spend less and less time with his wife and family, when he gives in to reading unwholesome literature, when he demonstrates unusually selfish behavior, beware. Something is happening to his character.

Cracks in the Shepherd's Ministry

Doctrinal Cracks. If a pastor begins to move away from sound teaching, there is great reason to be concerned. The lure to preach new fads and interesting pop psychology is always strong. Paul warns in 2 Timothy 4:3-4:

> For the time will come when men will not put up with sound doctrine. Instead, to suit their own desires, they will gather around them a great number of teachers to say what their itching ears want to hear. They will turn their ears away from the truth and turn aside to myths.

This ever-present danger demands that the minister feed the flock a balanced diet of biblical truth. Some sheep are like children—at times they want a diet that is not good for them. The pressure to give the flock what they want is relentless. Watch your shepherd. Keep him balanced.

Duty Cracks. Another sign of a staggering shepherd is weariness and the inability to persevere in the everyday duties of the pastorate. Paul instructs Timothy, "Do the work of an evangelist, discharge all the duties of your ministry" (2 Tim. 4:5). A pastor's commitment to prayer and to spiritual nourishment is usually the first thing to be abandoned. When he begins to show signs of physical and spiritual weariness, beware, he is vulnerable. He needs time away to recharge his batteries. Make him go!

192

Man-pleasing Cracks. A shepherd who is falling into both character and ministry aberrations will often demonstrate a dangerous habit of telling the congregation what they want to hear so their consciences will not be aroused. He may begin to espouse freedom from spiritual disciplines that are necessary for a godly lifestyle. "This promise of freedom may involve release from moral restraints, or a promise of release from the physical, financial or other limitations under which individuals may be called to live."[2] The full counsel of God's truth may be abandoned and replaced with a "love-only message."

I am familiar with one pastor in a large metropolitan city who preaches openly against the doctrine of the virgin birth and resurrection while moral purity and ethical righteousness are ridiculed! These are serious warning signs. By the way, his church is the largest in the city.

How easy it is for a man of God to experience cracks in his life and work. The signs of staggering are not easy to spot, especially if he wants them hidden. They seldom surface fully developed, but emerge in stages. If you see any of these hairline cracks developing, prayerfully express your concern to your shepherd. He'll be glad to know you're watching. Are you?

At the same time, we must be cautious not to be unfairly critical. Our desire is to build up, not to destroy. Our leaders live in a fishbowl where they are on display. They will make mistakes. But remember, they are also sinners saved by grace.

Three Keys to Keeping Your Shepherd On Track

God doesn't ask his sheep to read the minds of their pastors or overseers. But though it is impossible to monitor a shepherd's heart, internal struggles will eventually surface. What can be done to prevent much of the problems from germinating in the first place? What can the sheep do to protect the shepherd?

Over the years, I have developed a simple but effective process with the catchy acronym HAT:

H—keep your shepherd *humble*

A—keep your shepherd *accountable*

T—keep your shepherd *teachable*

Keep Your Shepherd Humble

Humility is the hallmark of the Christian faith. Peter exhorts all shepherds and sheep to be clothed with humility (1 Pet. 5:5). Paul gives a similar call for humility in Ephesians 4:2, "Be completely humble and gentle; be patient, bearing with one another in love." Humility was the Chief Shepherd's calling card (Matt. 11:29; 18:2-4; John 13:15). But most significantly, a humble spirit is the basis for a relationship with God: "God opposes the proud, but gives grace to the humble" (James 4:6).

When any Christian follows Christ's example of humility, God will give them added understanding, protection, and ultimately, responsibility. Only when we are humble can God trust us with his work. A shepherd who is arrogant will find himself resisted in the work of ministry.

How to Be Humble?

Many Christians consider a modest lifestyle the most important mark of humility. But humble lifestyle is not what James had in mind. Rather, humility is a condition of the spirit. How can sheep encourage a humble spirit in their shepherd?

First, *constant prayer*. While driving, resting, working—at any and all times—ask God for a humble shepherd. Believe me, God knows how to accomplish the task!

Remember that the pastor or elder has many heavy responsibilities that bring strain and stress and often invite self-reliance rather than a humble leaning on God. Humility will bring a sensitive spirit and heavenly help to the weighty job of being a shepherd. Surely that is the reason James wrote, "Not many of you should presume to be teachers, my brothers, because you know that we who teach will be judged more strictly" (3:1). Pray for your shepherd daily.

Watching Civil War movies has taught me how ridiculous warfare can be. Two armies line up seventy-five yards from each other, aim their weapons, and squeeze the trigger. Smoke clouds the sky, and those left standing reload and take a few steps forward for another try. It's good to remember that your shepherd is on the front lines of the spiritual battle and constantly in the enemy's sights. Without prayer, our leaders fight the battle at close range without proper protection. That is how the apostle Peter was attacked. "Simon, Simon, Satan has asked to sift you as wheat," said Jesus to Peter. "But I have prayed for you, Simon, that your faith may not fail" (Luke 22:31-32). Jesus knew that praying, even for the best men, was the only way to protect them.

Your pastor or shepherd will never be greater than *you* pray he will be.

Second, humility can be brought into a shepherd's life through *love demonstrations*. My home church had an annual ritual. On the anniversary of our pastor's call to our church, an all-church celebration was held. It was a "love-fest," and it was always initiated by a church member.

195

Everyone was invited to come and express love to the pastor and his wife and staff. Men, women, and children would express gratitude and thanksgiving to God for their shepherd. Many would bring gifts. Rather than making him proud, these demonstrations of love had the opposite effect: our pastor was always very humbled. He was never comfortable with the idea of focusing on him. He could see God at work through him . . . and that's humbling. By the way, the church held forty-two "love parties" for our pastor; he was our humble shepherd for over forty-two years.

On a weekly basis, every sheep can contribute to the humility of his shepherd through cards, telephone calls, and other creative ways of saying, "I love you." It lets him know that you're in the battle and that you believe God is using his gifts in your life. Try it this week.

Third, humility can be instilled in your minister through *submission to his leadership*. Many times, Christians are unconsciously defiant of their leaders, unwilling to submit to their teaching, ministry, or exhortation. But when sheep look to their shepherd for direction, it's humbling.

Several men in our church are my senior by fifteen to twenty years. These men often ask me, "Pastor, how can I pray for you this week?" Or, "Pastor, your ministry is important to me and this church. Stay sensitive to God." Every time one of these godly men calls me "pastor," I look over my shoulder to see who he is addressing. They show me such respect and so willingly submit to my leadership that it humbles me. Several times I have left their presence and sought a place to get on my knees, because I know they're expecting God to speak through me and lead his flock. Submit to your shepherd's ministry in your life and watch God humble his heart.

Keep Your Shepherd Accountable

Your shepherd needs to be held responsible for the direction of both his private life and public work. Howard Hendricks says a man of God needs more than just the knowledge that he is responsible to God. He also "needs somebody that has a face, that [he] can be accountable to right now, en route to that ultimate accountability."[3] Does your pastor have that "somebody with a face?"

Accountability involves asking the hard, penetrating questions about unseen areas in your leader's life. Charles Swindoll says, "It's the private, unseen things in the minister's life that make or break him."[4] Let's consider a few.

His marriage. How much time is your pastor spending with his wife? Is she still his heart's desire? These questions are close to home for me. An older brother in our fellowship asks me monthly, "When was the last time you took your wife out on a date?" Often it jars me back to the realization that I spend too few hours cultivating my relationship with my best friend . . . my wife.

His work schedule. It is commonplace for a pastor to work too many hours and keep a schedule that is so demanding, his family gets neglected. Often he will have little time to relax.

His physical health. What is your pastor doing to keep his body in shape? Does he have an exercise schedule? Sleep must also be kept in proper balance if he is to give 100 percent to his calling. Fatigued men are prone to make poor moral and ethical decisions.

His emotional health. Your pastor deals with many hurting people who drain him emotionally, making him a candidate for disappointment, depression, and anger. Emotional strength often comes through the encouragement of fellowship with close friends. The typical shepherd needs a few intimate friends both inside and outside his fellowship, if possible. People who love him unconditionally and encourage him are used by God to recharge his drained batteries. A pastor who takes time to cultivate close friends will avoid the dangers of isolation and emotional burnout.

His finances. Does your pastor have a budget? Is the church paying him enough to survive? Pastors need to be paid well and then be held accountable for proper handling of their income. Many ministers have made harmful decisions because they fell into the trap of overspending. The strain of heavy debt and poor spending habits can erode a work for God.

His spiritual health. The highest call of the shepherd is his relationship with Christ. At all costs, he must keep it intimate and strong. In these fast-paced times, it is easy to get caught up in day-to-day administrative duties. The tyranny of the urgent can keep your pastor from what is most important. He will have nothing of heaven's power to give on Sunday if he has not met alone with the Chief Shepherd during quiet hours of the week. Ask him about his prayer life and personal worship.

Most pastors love the church and work hard to see it grow. They start early in the morning and work late into the night. But a dangerous way of thinking can creep into the mind of a shepherd who is not under accountability. After a period, he can easily confuse "work" with "walk."

> Often a person is so busy in his activities that his attitudes deteriorate. The strength of a person's leadership on the outside is determined by the strength of his character within. You have to spend as much time cultivating your inner life as you do your external ministry.[5]

Time alone with the Chief Shepherd is essential, and yet spiritual nurture is usually last on the shepherd's "things to do" list.

When discussing why ministers fall, one author writes, "I have never seen one minister guilty of sexual sin who kept a daily personal devotion time in his walk with the Lord."[6] A man can pastor a large, growing church and be actively involved in sin and debauchery. There is no necessary correlation between godliness and church growth. Our nation has seen firsthand that men living in sin—men who confused their "work" of building a ministry with their "walk" with Christ—can have the fastest-growing ministry in the country one day and be behind bars the next.

Hold your shepherd accountable for keeping his walk with Christ his top priority. If he fails in his private life, often he fails publicly.

Not every sheep can assume the responsibility to hold his shepherd accountable. It takes a person close enough and bold enough to tackle the task. However, every believer should be sure that *someone* is routinely asking these hard questions. Do you know those people in your pastor's life?

Keep Your Shepherd Teachable

A pastor who is teachable is open to learning, changing, trying new ideas. Isolation can be stagnating. This teachable attitude comes about through training and cross-pollination with other men and ministries. You need to encourage your pastor to attend retreats, seminars, and conferences to keep new ideas and encouragements flowing. Frequent opportunities to learn and interact keep the shepherd aware of his and the church's needs. They keep him teachable!

I also suggest sabbatical rests. Often pastors need more than their annual vacation. Paul knew what the strain of ministry feels like: "We are hard pressed on every side" (2 Cor. 4:8). Pastors become disoriented when they minister nonstop at break-neck speed month after month. Spiritual fatigue will oppress any shepherd's life; he may need time away from the congregation to rest and renew his perspective. Pastors, like everyone else, need help avoiding job overload.

I recommend that churches follow the example of many academic institutions by allowing the pastor two to three months away every seven to ten years. Everyone will benefit. This time away is not just a vacation for basking on the beach, but rather an opportunity to dream about the future, reflect on the past, and pray himself back to full strength. It is amazing how much energy a pastor will bring back to his post, as well as how the rest of the church leadership will grow in his absence.

Teachable Moments for the Savior

Jesus went away to quiet places for relaxation and reflection. He had a place where the Father communicated with him and revealed direction for his work. He needed to rebuild his inner man after days of ministering to the crowds. If Jesus felt that need, how much more the shepherds of our flocks? Fatigued leaders lose teachability. They become isolated in their attempt to survive and often stop hearing from men or God.

> Local congregations need to recognize how crucial sabbatical breaks are for their leaders. We might even be surprised by fresh insights and perspectives wafting down from the pulpit. . . . [Those] on whose shoulders rests the responsibility

200

of maintaining Christian commitment amid the pressures of a secular world, should periodically step away from their "irreplaceable roles" to nurture and give direction to their personal commitments to God.[7]

A refreshed heart is usually a teachable heart.

In our effort to keep our shepherds on track, we should remember that God has provided the church with a secret weapon to be used in the morality arena. This weapon helps prevent counseling burnout and moral fissures in a pastor's life. This provision was given by God to protect the shepherd, yet the church today seldom calls on this resource.

The Church's Secret Weapon

We have an integrity crisis within the clergy. Some shepherds are giving in to their glands and giving up great gains in spiritual work for passions and possessions.

The typical demise is easy to plot. The pastor receives a phone call from a parishioner who is struggling in her marriage or from a recent divorce. Her private life is broken to pieces and she needs emotional support. A counseling appointment is made . . . and she returns week after week for her emotional fix. After a time, he finds himself looking forward to their meetings. Then his mental energy centers around his special counseling appointment. Eventually, he is out of the ministry and, often, his marriage is ruined.

Is a pastor responsible to meet all the needs of the women in his flock who suffer from relational cracks? No. The shepherd should approach with caution such dangerous situations. God has provided another safe and effective means for meeting these needs.

Older Christian Women, Apply Here

Paul understood the marvelous resource God has given to the church when he writes to the older women:

> Likewise, teach the older women to be reverent in the way they live, not to be slanderers or addicted to much wine, but to teach what is good. Then they can train the younger women to love their husbands and children, to be self-controlled and pure, to be busy at home, to be kind, and to be subject to their husbands, so that no one will malign the word of God (Titus 2:3-5)

Older women in the church are a powerful resource to nurture younger women, to assist them during difficult times, and to set an example of godliness.

The term "older women" refers more to maturity than to age. A mature female disciple of Christ has much to offer her local church. She has lived through many experiences and received her "diploma of life." She has God's credentials. She has been a servant in the body of Christ, raised children, been a money manager, suffered heartache and sometimes loss. She has learned home management skills, marriage skills, perhaps managed a career, and observed how easy it is for mistakes to damage a life. *She is God's provision for the women in the church.*

The mature women in our fellowship deserve to do more for God's kingdom than prepare potluck dinners. They need to be encouraged to assume other ministries, including the high calling of ministering to other women. Many of the young mothers in our church do not have the much-needed encouragement of a mother living close by. Older women can give those younger women counsel and experienced help. They understand emotional needs and usually have the ability to establish a long-term relationship. It's a sacred duty that a pastor, though he may be sympathetic, is less qualified to do. What a great resource!

It is sad how absent the older women's influence is in the modern church. It's a glaring weakness, pointing out that the defensive mechanism God built into the church is undeveloped, eroding, or neglected. As a result, everyone is vulnerable . . . especially the man up front.

The older women need to be available. It is one of God's built-in safeguards. Older women are not called to minister to the younger in order to avoid bringing the pastor into disrepute; rather, the pastor's protection is simply a by-product of an effective women's ministry. Without placing blame on the women, I have often wondered how many shepherds would still be in charge of their flocks, how many marriages would still be intact, how great the army of maturing young women would be, if the older saints took up the challenge. As the psalmist says:

> They will still bear fruit in old age,
>   they will stay fresh and green
>   (Ps. 92:14).

Our Desperate Need

Marie Fortune makes a shocking observation about sin and Christian leadership today:

> The profession of the ministry will continue to lose its credibility until it becomes one of the least-respected professions in our society. These are the tragic consequences of the unethical behavior of the few. . . . Although this issue has existed for years, the church has refused to prepare itself to deal with it.[8]

What should the church be doing to deal with the problem? Does God's Word give direction for returning credibility and respect to the church today? What should you do if *your* shepherd fails? The guidelines from God might catch most Christians offguard.

Notes

1. Richard Dobbins, "Why Do Ministers Fall?" *Ministries Today Magazine*, May/June 1989, 24.

2. Larry Richards, *When the People You Trust Let You Down*, (Waco, Tex.: Word Books, 1987), 39.

3. Howard G. Hendricks cited in Dan Mitchum, "How to Restore Integrity," *Dallas Insider Magazine*, Fall 1989, 3.

4. Charles Swindoll cited in ibid., 2.

5. Hendricks cited in ibid., 3.

6. Dobbins, "Why Do Ministers Fall?" 24.

7. F. LeGard Smith, *Fallen Shepherds, Scattered Sheep* (Eugene, Ore.: Harvest House Publishers, 1988), 189.

8. Marie M. Fortune, *Is Nothing Sacred?* (San Francisco: Harper & Row Publishers, 1989), 107.

CHAPTER TWELVE

Confronting the Fallen Shepherd:
What to Do If Yours Fails!

I have a weak spot for the fine art of quail hunting. It is hard to resist a crisp, dew-kissed morning with the sun at my back and a well-trained dog on point. I know I'm fully alive every time I hear the thunder of a rising covey. Now that's excitement! Along with the therapy of the outdoors comes good conversation with hunting partners. Opportunities to go are rare, so I seldom pass them up.

Like the time a friend in our church offered me a day in the field hunting behind two champion breed dogs. While checking my schedule (there was never any question), he told me the dogs belonged to an old friend he wanted me to meet. The idea of a new friendship built around some quality hunting time . . . well, I was ready!

When my friend finally picked me up for the hunt,

one quick glance revealed that it was just the two of us and a couple of untrained backyard mutts. Disappointed about the change in plans, I asked, "What happened?" His response was not straightforward. I had to read between the lines, and when I finally understood, it was hurtful. His friend had refused to come when he learned a preacher would be on the hunt. After two loved and respected pastors abandoned their churches and families and left town with their secretaries, this long-time follower of Christ had given up the faith, dropped out of church, and abandoned his life of service to the Lord. Neither pastor was disciplined for his actions. This friend had been through a lot, and he was disappointed and reluctant to trust any minister. It was hard for me to blame him.

Our dogs never made a point that day, but the tragic story of a disappointed life and two undisciplined leaders did!

Warning: Religious Stories Can Be Shocking

In a nearby city, a young wife lies comatose from a brutal late-night assault. The police have been unable to solve the mystery, but the evidence points toward her husband . . . a well-known spiritual leader in that city.

In another city just a few miles to the south, the pastor of a large fellowship has been expelled for homosexual activity. Only a few years ago, the church leaders confronted the problem, hid it from the congregation, and warned him twice. What else could they do? Now the sin was back with a vengeance, and this time as front-page news.

We must stop defending ourselves and admit it—a great fraternity of leaders are exposing their feet of clay. Some are good men or women whose integrity was lost. Others are deceivers whose lack of integrity was exposed.

Some are genuine, others phony, but the danger is still the same. What should the church do if their leaders fall into sin? The church needs some tough answers for these tough situations.

Handling the Sinning Servant

It is easy to forget that a pastor is also a member of the church. He is subject to care and discipline like any other member. His station does entitle him to honor and respect—and to certain cautions that I will discuss later—but he is not exempt from discipline.

Disciplining a pastor or key leader is a sobering thought for any church official. The one who has faithfully led the ministry and shown such a zeal for the things of God is not easily approached by those who have seen him as God's "called" leader. It's a hard process to consider—so hard that those responsible for taking the disciplinary action often become "under-the-rug sweepers." They argue for leaving the situation alone and letting God handle the problem in his own time and way. The church may fear that if it exposes the leader's sin, the ministry may be dampened or destroyed. Or the church may feel that it can't get along without him. "Who will organize and lead with such power and authority? What embarrassment we will have to suffer if we expose his failing!"

However, this loving responsibility does not go away. The leader must be confronted and, if necessary, disciplined.

Does the New Testament give clear direction on how to discipline a fallen leader? Yes . . . but not without the apostle Paul's bold caution, WARNING, HANDLE WITH CARE.

Danger: Proceed with Caution!

Just as a high standard of integrity is required of those in church leadership (1 Tim. 3:1-13; Titus 1:5-9), so also a high standard is set for churches faced with the difficult task of restoring a key figure. The discipline of a leader should be handled, at least in the initial stages, like the discipline of any other member (Matt. 18:15f). However, if steps one and two have failed or if the offense is already public, the discipline of the leader must take a distinct twist.

Paul's teaching on the proper care and handling of a fallen (or accused) leader is given in 1 Timothy 5:19-21. In these three verses, he gives three strong cautions:

1. Never accept an accusation without significant proof (1 Tim. 5:19).

Paul says at the beginning of chapter 5, "Do not rebuke an older man harshly, but exhort him as if he were your father." This is the spirit that should govern the initial steps in disciplining a leader. After steps one and two of Matthew 18 have been attempted without success, then the matter should be brought before the other ruling authorities of the fellowship. This might be another elder or an entire board of overseers. To these, Paul writes:

> Do not entertain an accusation against an elder unless it is brought by two or three witnesses (5:19).

People with high visibility are often attacked unjustly. Knowing that leaders suffer from such attacks, distorted perceptions, and false accusations, Paul warned the church to move with the greatest caution. Strong evidence of misconduct is required, because critics can start a brushfire of rumors if precautions are not taken.

Good Reasons for Good Facts

There are two principal reasons for taking elaborate precautions. First, taking precautions protects all parties from Satan's attacks; he will rush through any window of opportunity to arouse controversy. It is advisable to act quickly and to handle the problem in a small group of leaders before discussing it with the congregation. Gossip, which flies on wings when it concerns a person in the public eye, can damage the leader and the whole fellowship. The better known and more widely respected the leader, the more spicy the gossip and the greater the temptation to spread it. Even if the leader did not succumb to temptation, his or her downfall could be brought about by gossip alone.

Second, if there is no significant proof of the accusation, abandon the matter only after carrying the facts and findings back to the witnesses or the accusers. Then require their silence!

The next warning may come as a surprise, but Paul wanted to spare the church from making the most dangerous mistake in discipline today.

2. Never hide the sin from the congregation (1 Tim. 5:20).

If the accusations brought forth by the witnesses prove undeniably true, then some discipline is necessary. Attempting to avoid public disclosure of a leader's sin is a common mistake, but being obedient to the biblical guidelines is essential for the health of the *entire* fellowship. So Paul tells us, "get it out in the open."

> Those who sin are to be rebuked publicly, so that the others may take warning (5:20).

The caution is straightforward: The sin is to be made

public. Due to the visibility of a leader and his heavy responsibility, the failure must be shared with the members of the church. Even though it may seem more fitting to hide the wrongs . . . don't!

Public rebuke is set in contrast to paying double honor to a faithful elder (1 Tim. 5:17). Those "who direct the affairs of the church well" is contrasted with "those who sin." Shepherds who discharge their duties with zeal and righteousness deserve extra honor. Any overseer who defaults on his duties for Christ is to be publicly revealed, receiving *dishonor.*

What if the errant leader has confessed and repented of his sin? A public acknowledgment and confession is still required. No distinction is made in Paul's mind: Proven sin demands a public announcement. Certainly the apostle is not calling for public exposure for the shepherd's eating six pieces of pumpkin pie at Aunt Bessie's on Thanksgiving. The sin should be of a serious nature and constitute a violation of the pastor's office and calling. Publicly exposed sins should be those that act as a detriment to the pastor's ministry, family, or character. This unusual command is a secret weapon of protection for those who accept it.

But if the sinning shepherd has a contrite and repentant heart, is it necessary to drag his reputation and his family into the public light? Yes, for several critical reasons.

Purposes for Public Acknowledgment

The first reason for bringing the failure to the church is not to shame or humiliate the exposed leader, but that "the others may take warning" (v. 20). Discipline encourages each believer to examine his life. It acts as a spiritual cleanser on the congregation, encouraging a healthy attitude toward sin and its consequences. Also, public confession demonstrates a high level of integrity in the pastor's life. Doing the difficult thing builds strength, character, and respect.

I have learned to take seriously Paul's warning. My own pragmatic personality inclines me to argue, If a leader's sin mars his life and ministry, then quietly release him from his duties and encourage him to leave the area. Seeking another place to carry on his life seems more sensible than erecting a neon display of his wrongdoings in front of the church. If he repents and confesses, then keeping the matter quietly hidden would seem to be the healthiest plan for everyone.

However, if we fail to bring the problem before the church, the enemy will take what we believe is buried in the past and blaze it in bold red letters on his own neon billboard. False accusations and gossip will spread and contaminate the people. Far more damage will be done when a leader's sins are not handled publicly. Hiding sin brings dangerous consequences to the entire ministry.

When Sheep Fill in the Blanks

When church members are uninformed and left to fill in the blanks themselves, they often make false assumptions that can be devastating not only to the church but also to the rest of the leadership. Bill Hybels, pastor of one of the largest churches in the country, experienced the results of the "wheels coming off" when a cofounder of the church fell into sin and the decision was made to keep the matter quiet. The leadership felt that a simple announcement that the copastor was resigning would be sufficient. Laurie Pederson writes about the backwash:

> Well, after the service, people just went nuts. They said, "What in the world is going on? This guy is a genius, he is one of the founders of the

church and he is your best friend. What's *really* going on?"

Because the elders and Hybels did not feel free to discuss all the issues—namely, [the copastor's] sin—many people made this assumption: Bill Hybels was making a power play. Many were already aware that Hybels had changed his title to senior pastor.

It was like a bomb went off after that announcement. Within twenty-four hours people had taken sides.

The elders, as it turned out, had made another incorrect assumption. Says Dr. Bilezikian: "We thought people would trust our judgment, so we didn't go into the details. As a result, people began to accuse the elders of taking sides with Bill and trying to run [the copastor] out of the church."

The fallout was devastating. Some people left the church immediately. Many stayed and "stared bullets." The idea of community, which for so long had marked the church, was becoming a memory. Instead of "us," it was "us" versus "them."

"The best way I can describe it," Hybels says, "is that the wheels just came off. Instead of community drawing closer together, there was a splintering of community."[1]

Never hide sin from the congregation. Though it seems honorable to protect the leader's integrity, it brings an acidic backwash into the church. When faithful, a shepherd is to receive double honor; when unfaithful, double exposure!

How to Rebuke Publicly

The public rebuke of a leader is no picnic. However, if handled with love and care, it can be a safeguard against confusion and distrust, and in some instances, a public opportunity for confession and healing. A community rebuke of a fallen leader could follow one of three scenarios.

An Empty Seat. The transgressing leader with an unrepentant spirit will most often refuse to attend the open meeting. Usually he has removed himself from the consequences and the shame of his actions. In this case, the acting leaders should reveal only the necessary facts of the misdeed and instruct the members about the removal of the leader's responsibilities and the lifting of his ordination. The church members will often need to ask questions as they seek understanding and personal healing. Other meetings for continued healing may be necessary until the process seems complete.

A Drawn Sword. Unfortunately, a leader with skill and charisma, who is loved by the people, could use the public rebuke as a platform for a fight. In some situations, the unrepentant leader could possess such authority that he turns the meeting into a debate over his guilt, which could cause a church split. Leaders have been known to recruit members to support them in an open meeting. This scheme can do significant damage to the spiritual balance of a congregation.

As I said earlier, accusations against the leader should be handled in private before the public rebuke. A select committee should investigate the charges and determine the direction of the pastor's future before the issue is brought before the church. If a struggle for power arises, those who brought the evidence of wrongdoing to the leaders of the fellowship must be prepared to restate the truth before the congregation. The acting leaders should not allow the meeting to become an emotional battleground for the venting of anger, frustration, or vengeance, nor should it become a forum for cross-examination.

A Contrite Heart. When the pastor privately repents to those who have investigated the transgression, the public meeting should be only a time of confession and healing. If the pastor is willing to confess his wrongdoing, revealing only the necessary details, and ask for forgiveness, extraordinary healing often follows. The congregation is free to express forgiveness and demonstrate their love and support during this difficult time. The opportunity is priceless for the leader and his people. In many cases he is able to continue on with his ministry with a renewed commitment to accountability.

The Ingredients of a Public Confession

The ingredients of a public confession are illustrated by King David in Psalm 51: sincere acknowledgment, a heart-felt expression of repentance, and a desire for forgiveness. This simple formula is a good guideline for the public confession of any leader.

If confession has taken place, the church should lovingly set about to restore and heal the leader. This may mean his removal from office or the removal of his ordination until restoration is complete. If necessary, professional counseling should begin. Each situation will be unique, but whatever the direction, it can be done in harmony and love and for everyone's benefit. (I will discuss the restoration process more thoroughly in the next chapter.)

There is one final warning that is easy to accept but hard to do.

3. Never show partiality toward the leader (1 Tim. 5:21).

Any loving associate or board member charged with disciplining a fellow minister will have to agonize over the tendency to show partiality. Men who have prayed together, played together, worked together, or who share a common philosophy of ministry will lean over backward to help an associate suffering in pain and spiritual defeat. It almost seems as though Paul experienced the same struggle when he warns:

> I charge you, in the sight of God and Christ Jesus and the elect angels, to keep these instructions without partiality, and to do nothing out of favoritism (5:21).

Paul commands every believer involved to check his emotional tie to the transgressing leader. In the exercise of discipline, we must be careful, precise, methodical, objective, and honest every grueling step of the way.

> The discipline of Christian leaders is to be judicious and impartial. A leader, because of sentiment, should not be subject to lighter discipline than another person. It is very easy to respond with our emotions and be more generous in dealing with a leader we love and admire than with others. Probably in no other situation do we see such an expression of our human weakness, either in being overly harsh or in being overly lenient. Those involved in administering church discipline must be neither.[2]

Discipline and the Fallen Leader

A visual of the proper steps may help in understanding the biblical process:

WHAT TO DO IF YOUR LEADER FAILS
1 Timothy 5:19-22

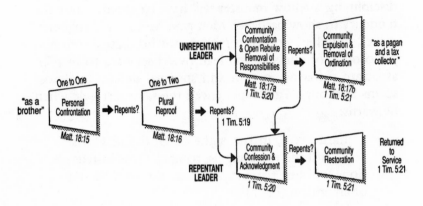

Those asked to navigate such rocky waters might ask, "Why subject myself to the stress?" The answer calms our fears: The leader's life is worth the effort, the bride of Christ and her purity is worth the effort, and our Lord demands the effort. Great leaders come forth from such fiery battles.

At times we need to be reminded that those called to the task are given supernatural help during the grinding process. Jesus will be present with his divine wisdom and grace (Matt. 18:19-20). He promised!

A Cooked Turkey

I'm amazed at many of our modern-day conveniences. One small example is the plastic device often placed in a turkey to tell the cook when the bird is done. When the meal is cooked, the indicator pops up.

Each year since 1986, a major national figure has fallen

into sin and public embarrassment. These failings, and other, less publicized ones, are indicators of the church's lack of integrity and tolerance of sin. These indicators will continue to pop up, for below the placid surface of the Christian faith today great contamination exists.

But once that sin has been exposed and properly disciplined, what next? What about restoration? Is there hope for a future, or is it to the graveyard for burned out and fallen shepherds?

Notes

1. Laurie Pederson, *Willow Creek Community Church Magazine*, Special 15th Anniversary Issue, December 1990, 36.

2. Carl Laney, *A Guide to Church Discipline* (Minneapolis: Bethany House Publishers, 1985), 122.

CHAPTER THIRTEEN

Restoring the Fallen Shepherd

How should the church treat leaders who have openly demonstrated their humanity? Should we view them as one of life's tragedies and remove them from the church family portrait? How should the church respond after confrontations and confessions are over?

Fellowships today typically respond in three ways to the plight of a fallen pastor.

Sweep it under the rug. Some of the key leadership may know about the pastor's struggle in sin, but they choose to blindly trust his future actions now that he has been caught. The remaining church members are not informed.

Pass the pastor, please. Others play the popular "pass the pastor" game. It is a game of secrecy in which the sin is covered up. Then the shepherd is quietly encouraged to pursue his next ministry opportunity . . . quickly. Later, when he again falls, the next church discovers that they were unsuspecting victims of a cover-up.

Forgive and forget. In this case, the congregation is somehow informally or formally made aware of the pastor's predicament. Forgiveness is bestowed upon the pastor, and the life in the fellowship continues as if the sin has no effect on the church members or the pastor.

Love for the pastor is supposedly the motivating factor behind each of these actions. Yet in each situation, the pastor is the real loser. One of the greatest weaknesses in the Kingdom today is the failure to restore fallen leaders. "Leadership rebuilding" should be high priority. The Christian community needs to come to the bedside of stricken leaders and get involved in the healing process. Hebrews 12 tells us the Lord disciplines those he loves that we may share in his holiness. Real love demands restoration.

Defining Restoration

The church working toward restoration must desire to return the pastor to his original condition as a Christian and as a servant-leader. He needs a new beginning.

Two levels of restoration are necessary for the shepherd—the restoration of his fallen relationship with God (spiritual restoration) and restoration to his place of ministry (positional restoration). Both are essential since his calling to spiritual leadership came out of his relationship to God. But restoration to a place of ministry can never happen apart from his restoration to God. He must be right with God first.

The fallen leader lives under the same grace as all

other Christians. Heartfelt repentance brings forgiveness and restoration to God (2 Sam. 12:13; 1 John 1:9). When true repentance and deep sorrow come over the leader, he needs the encouragement of the flock to assure him that he has truly been forgiven. Christians should never avoid nor treat with disdain a repentant leader. He needs to be loved and consoled now more than ever, since he could easily be consumed by grief and despair.

In 2 Corinthians 2:7 the church is told to forgive and comfort the repentant offender in order to avoid his emotional destruction. We should be ready to restore just as soon as the erring brother has passed the test of repentance. However, the church must realize that forgiveness is not synonymous with restoration. To bring the fallen to complete healing and avoid the same aftershock later in his life, he needs not only to be forgiven, but also restored.

But what if he does confess and repent, and the challenge of restoration is accepted? How should the process unfold?

GETTING THE JOB DONE: HOW SHOULD THE RESTORATION TAKE PLACE?

Most denominations have codes for the rebuilding of fallen leaders. In many cases, the process is handled by appointed boards or committees, but restoration always calls for the involvement of all caring members of the body of Christ. Below, I have summarized some of the specific action steps that should be taken.

General Guidelines

To begin spiritual restoration and movement back toward full-time ministry, this list of attitudes and actions should be demonstrated:

- Genuine repentance and contrition
- Willingness to meet with the overseers
- Acceptance of a plan for rehabilitation
- No public ministry without overseers' approval
- Willingness to accept counseling
- Willingness to submit to a pastor or mentor
- No reoccurrence of the problem sin.[1]

Credentials

Most ministers are required to submit to ordination testing and other ministerial requirements. These credentials may be temporarily removed by those responsible for the healing process. A leader's restoration and full reinstatement to his original post might require retesting and reordination after he has completed a period of observation. Formal recognition of restoration and reinstatement would be encouraging to all parties.

Adding Responsibilities

The restoration process will take planning and overseeing new ministry and work-related responsibilities. The leader will need to begin to rebuild his life and confidence in small, well-defined steps.

> This can be accomplished by giving responsibilities at various levels, beginning with the lowest. As the repentant leader proves himself faithful in the accomplishment of those responsibilities, he can be advanced upwards. But beware of advancing the person beyond the point where he has the trust and respect of subordinates in the organization.[2]

Restoration demands a spirit of humility and willingness to serve God in any way.

Time: Looking at the Finish Line

How long will the restoration process take? As long as necessary to bring observable readiness and proven character qualities to the leader's life. This takes time. Those who have fallen and been quickly reinstated have been done an injustice.

The time requirements depend upon the nature of the sin and the attitude of the sinner. It may take as long as it took the leader to achieve his office. Enough time is needed for the errant brother to prove himself to the community, the congregation, and the church leadership. In his article, "How to Restore the Fallen," Almon Bartholomew describes the time sequence necessary to bring one denominational shepherd back to full-time ministry.

> The minister was not allowed public ministry for the first year. He was gradually phased into ministry at the church he attended during the second year. After two years, he was completely restored.
>
> After two years, this minister's suspension was lifted and he was assisted in finding a place of ministry. He and his family are doing well and are respected among their peers.
>
> He and his wife are now serving faithfully and effectively in a pastoral ministry.[3]

Reputation

A leader's relationship with his church is only part of the rebuilding process. For the shepherd to assume his original place of leadership, he needs a good reputation with outsiders (1 Tim. 3:7); that reputation must be regained as much as possible before he can be restored.

Community reputation is an intangible that is hard to evaluate. However, with enough time and opportunities to rebuild it, the leader should have won some renewed respect outside his church.

The board responsible for reinstatement should make some attempt to evaluate the errant brother's reputation before he is returned. His attempt to rebuild should have caught the attention of some in the community.

Overcoming the Weakness

Before a fallen shepherd can be restored, he should also show consistent moral victory in his area of weakness. Some use the restoration of Peter as a guideline. After the resurrection, Jesus asked Peter three times to confess his love for him . . . the same number of times Peter denied that he knew Jesus the night of his arrest (John 21:15-17). Proven faithfulness in the area of one's weakness is suggested by this incident. Before a fallen shepherd can be restored, respect and trust in the area of his weakness must also be restored. Has he proven he can overcome temptation in the area where he has known his greatest struggle and failure?

Parachurch Discipline

For those in Christian organizations and parachurch ministries, the authorities over the work should develop similar procedures. As to who makes the decisions and how they should be made, Carl Laney writes:

> In Christian organizations, the officers or board must make the decisions. In order to avoid internal conflict due to a lack of trust or respect for a former co-worker, it would be wise for the administrative officers or board to make such

crucial decisions with counsel and input from the other workers in the organization.[4]

Can a Pastor be Permanently Removed?

Full restoration of a pastor to his previous place of service is not only the goal but also the logical outcome of discipline. Some sins are more serious and cause deeper cracks than others (embezzling church funds, for example, would cause more difficulty than alcohol abuse) and the status and visibility of a leader's place of service is important to the restoration process. But full reinstatement to the original office could and should take place.

Is There a Ministry Back Shelf?

In almost every home, there is a place reserved for household items that are either outdated or no longer fit the decor of the home. These items may be used again some day for other purposes, but for now they find a resting place on the back shelf. As difficult as it may seem, God does have a back shelf in his kingdom.

Paul knew of God's back shelf, and he openly feared it for the future of his service to God: "I beat my body and make it my slave so that after I have preached to others, I myself will not be disqualified for the prize" (1 Cor. 9:27). The great apostle knew there was always potential for disqualification from the ministry. Every shepherd faces the possibility of sinning in such a manner that he could no longer serve God in a previous position of trust.

Loss of a position is a possibility, yet it should be remembered that sinlessness is not a prerequisite for service in the Kingdom of God. Not one of the apostles was sinless. That a minister is called to a blameless lifestyle does not mean he is without sin; rather, his life truly represents

God and meets the biblical requirements for a shepherd. His life must be one of highest caliber, but moral perfection is not possible.

God does not demand that we be sinless to hold a place of service. He demands that all sin be dealt with through genuine, heartfelt repentance and forgiveness. True, some sins leave deeper, more visible scars that can delay for some time a leader's return to service. But these do not necessarily signal "permanent disqualification."

Four Paths Away from Reinstatement

Even though restoration is the aim, a leader can find himself disqualified, not by a specific category of sin, but by four other possible means.

First, God can permanently remove from service one of his servants. Moses had received the Ten Commandments, led the people of Israel for forty years in the desert, and spent hours in God's presence. Yet, one act of disobedience was such an affront that God disqualified him from service and entrance into the land of promise (Deut. 32:48-52). Even though his relationship to God was restored, Moses' failure placed him on the back shelf. God communicated this to Moses directly. Today, I believe this transaction occurs between the spirit of the servant and the Spirit of God; unfortunately, all too often the servant is unwilling to listen.

Second, a leader might be set aside permanently by a formal decision of those in authority over him. Many in the ministry have placed themselves under a board for accountability, fellowship, and spiritual protection. In such cases, the fallen leader should be humble enough to submit to the established authority structure rather than disowning it.

One nationally known televangelist fell into disgrace and grieved his ministry and the entire Christian community. After his public confession of guilt and plea for forgiveness, his denomination placed him on leave of absence from his ministry for several months. However, he refused to step down from his ministry duties and follow the guidelines of proper conduct. Instead, he left his denomination.

If a man is ordained by a denomination or an independent fellowship and he confesses allegiance to their authority, he should submit or find himself no longer qualified to represent that ministry. It is important that ministry heads be cautious about the restoration process. Returning an errant brother to an office of high and sacred trust when he is not submissive communicates that God is not really concerned with maintaining holiness.

Third, leaders are judged by higher standards (James 3:1). Even though repentance and forgiveness may occur, some sins render the pastor no longer "above reproach" (1 Tim. 3:2). A shepherd is disqualified if he does not meet the high standards of godly leadership stated in 1 Timothy 3:1-7 and Titus 1:6-9.

> Ultimately, if a person is walking with Christ and has demonstrated maturity, and meets the requirements of 1 Timothy 3 and other related passages, then there is no past sin that should bar him from office. If, however, the past sin has continuing ramifications, as in the case of a man who can't control his family, then this should be considered in light of the leadership passages.[5]

Fourth, any fallen leader who refuses to acknowledge his error and seek forgiveness and restoration in God's eyes is given a permanent pink slip. The blood of Christ covers all our sins and mistakes, yet repentance is essential for restoration. A leader who leaves one ministry under a cloud of rebellion and starts another without confessing his error and pursuing restoration is acting in defiance. Even though he may carry on "a work" for God, he is "ineligible." A sprinter might finish a race with the fastest time, yet if he runs out of his lane, he is disqualified. A minister who has stepped out of bounds may still be running, but he will forfeit the race.

One writer sums up this argument: "It is not the sin that a man commits that determines whether or not he has a further place in God's service, but his response when he is confronted with his sin. There is a delicate balance between grace and truth."[6]

Comparing Apples to Oranges

Many disagree with the premise that a fallen leader might suffer permanent removal. They argue that the Bible is full of men who failed and yet experienced complete restoration to their previous place of service. Many of these men had fruitful ministries after their involvement in serious sin. Certainly King David is a favorite. Even after adultery and murder, David was forgiven and restored, and he is often cited as a biblical pattern and justification for any leader's full restoration to service.

However, comparing David to a minister of the gospel is like comparing apples to oranges: It is a category mistake. David was a king. He was the hero of the nation and the key political figure, but he was not the spiritual mediator over Israel. The priests held that post. The minister of today is parallel to the priests of old. David should not be used as a biblical pattern for the restoration of a contemporary priest (1 Pet. 2:5) who serves under the eternal high priest, Christ Jesus our Lord.

A Double Standard

Others who disagree with the possibility of permanent removal feel if other Christians can find forgiveness for their sins and restoration to places of service, anything less for the pastor represents a double standard. Christ's death paid for all sin equally. However, James informs us that men and women called into positions of ministry to represent a Holy God are judged more seriously: "Not many of you should presume to be teachers, my brothers, because you know that we who teach will be judged more strictly" (James 3:1).

The office teachers and leaders hold reflects to the world God's character and holy nature. Easy restoration can communicate to Christians and non-Christians alike that God is not concerned with holiness, but only with mercy and forgiveness. Man cannot violate God's laws and expect the consequences to be a simple slap on the hand.

Confusing Restoration with Forgiveness

Forgiveness and restoration are not always synonymous in the Kingdom of God. The Christian community should avoid the attitude that forgiveness has not been truly extended to an erring leader until he is fully restored to his previous office. God loves and forgives every repentant fallen leader, but under certain conditions full reinstatement may not be possible.

The withholding of a position of recognized leadership under those circumstances is not a commentary on one's personal acceptability in the eyes of God or the church. Nor does failure to reinstate him officially prevent him from going about informally doing the work of a spiritual leader. But giving him a badge of approval when the world is looking on with scorn can only be a stumbling block to their potential faith in God who calls us to uncompromised holiness.[7]

Finding Other Options

Every leader has been given gifts the church needs. Before closing the door on a fallen leader's full return to service, other alternatives should be explored.

If one is to be banned from the pulpit, for example, is there no teaching role he can fill? If, for a time, one is unsuitable as a teacher, might he not become a counselor to others, who are his fellow sinners? If public interaction seems inadvisable, is there something behind the scenes to which he could contribute? The leader's sin is disgrace enough. We don't need to compound the disgrace by throwing away sorely-needed skills or, worse yet, a precious soul.[8]

Encouragement for the Fallen and Those Who Love Them

On the road to recovery, the fallen leader often experiences hurt and confusion. These emotions are expressed in this open letter from a restored minister:

You've disappointed those who believed in you. You've lost your present ministry. You've severely wounded your mate. You sit alongside Job on his ash heap and scrape your sores with the broken potsherds of the past.[9]

The anonymous letter encourages other shepherds passing

through that dark valley to remember three principles in the midst of their pain:

> First, recognize the validity of the truths you have preached to others. God forgives and forgets. Don't castigate yourself. You ask forgiveness and our Father, who cannot lie, has forgiven you. Be willing to forgive yourself.
>
> Second, be strong. Don't expect God to deliver you from these trials of your own making, but do expect Him to give you more grace, more courage, more stamina. Be resolute.
>
> Third, be determined. You got yourself into this mess, you made the choice. Now you must make a better choice. Determine to be a better man, a better husband, a better father, a better minister. Submit your will to God and to those He's appointed over you.
>
> Last, understand God's design behind the disciplinary process. Hebrews 12:5-6 (NIV) reminds us: "My son, do not make light of the Lord's discipline, and do not lose heart when he rebukes you, because the Lord disciplines those he loves."
>
> Because He loves you, He corrects you. Later your pain will turn to quiet joy and solid gratitude to God. I thank God for this rehabilitation period. I am a better man than I was two years ago.[10]

It takes desire, commitment, and a well-developed plan before God's people can celebrate restoration. To see a servant of God once again walking with Christ and prepared for a return to his place of service is well worth the effort. What a victory!

Restoration demonstrates to God that the church is serious about its mandate to love one another. It lifts leaders from the depths of disgrace and places them back in the light of grace.

These principles apply to anyone who has served in a leadership position. He should be restored, forgiven, and placed back in service as soon as the healing is evident. From his life will come a measure of mercy and compassion that only a dark experience such as he's suffered can teach. Let's get on with the task of restoration.

"I will not accuse forever,
    nor will I always be angry,
for then the spirit of man would grow faint
        before me—
the breath of man that I have created.
. . . .
I have seen his ways, but I will heal him;
    I will guide him and restore comfort to him
                            (Is. 57:16, 18).

Notes

1. Almon M. Bartholomew, "How to Restore the Fallen," *Ministries Today,* Jan-Feb 1988, 32.

2. Carl Laney, *A Guide to Church Discipline* (Minneapolis: Bethany House Publishers, 1985), 162.

3. Bartholomew, "How to Restore the Fallen," 32.

4. Laney, *Guide to Church Discipline,* 162.

5. Ronald N. McKay, "Service after Sin for Pastors" (Unpublished paper, Dallas Theological Seminary, 1984), 1-3, 12-15.

6. Gordon F. Schroeder, "An Analysis of Current Practice of Church Discipline among Churches Pastored by Graduates of Dallas Theological Seminary" (D. Min. diss., Dallas Theological Seminary, 1986), 77.

7. F. LeGard Smith, *Fallen Shepherds, Scattered Sheep* (Eugene, Ore.: Harvest House Publishing, 1988), 174.

8. Ibid., 177.

9. Cited in Bartholomew, "How to Restore the Fallen," 32.

10. Ibid.

Standing on Shaky Ground

Nothing could be more fatuous than the belief that a people reborn to a living hope could possibly exist without a tough, resilient discipline. The body of Christ has structure, a skeleton that gives it leverage so that it can make a difference in the world. But the American church is an amoeba.
—Fred Cervin

Lack of discipline is a sign of miserable weakness in the church.—Emil Bruner

The church that bears the name of Christ stands at a crossroad. Sin has eroded her integrity. From the top leadership to the last person in the pew, purity is no longer a priority. The church is threatened more by internal contamination and impurity than by any outside force.

The earthquakes that rumble from within have also shattered much of the church's influence on our fragile and needy world. As evangelicals, we are in danger of losing credibility when we speak out on moral issues, because the distinction of Christ's bride is dissolving. The church has fallen into the trap of being more concerned about the less significant: enlistment of new members, fund raising, and comfortable, attractive buildings.

Not One of the Non-Essentials

Because we stand on such shaky ground, it becomes even more urgent that we return to the New Testament doctrines that Jesus gave to keep his church healthy and holy. The experience of the New Testament church demonstrates that church discipline is essential. In fact, Paul demonstrated more anger toward the church at Corinth for its failure to discipline a rebellious believer than he did toward the errant believer himself (1 Cor. 5:1-5). The resurrected Jesus reproved the church at Pergamum and Thyatira for neglecting to exercise discipline (Rev. 2:14,15,20).

Rightly administered, discipline is a God-honoring exercise that will bring peace, unity, and power back to the church. Reformer John Calvin recognized its value when he said, "Therefore, all who desire to remove discipline or to hinder its restoration, whether they do this deliberately or out of ignorance, are surely contributing to the dissolution of the church." Without corrective discipline, the church is in danger of ceasing to be *the church*. Discipline is not one of the non-essentials.

A Key to Spiritual Renewal

Discipline can return strength and vigor to the church in America. Church historian Winthrop S. Hudson writes, "Thus far it is clear from church history that an indispensable prerequisite to the renewal of the church as a dynamic force in American life is the recovery of corrective church discipline."[1]

One of the more striking observations in American church life today is the correlation between discipline and spiritual and numerical growth.[2] The biblical account of Ananias and Sapphira illustrates the principle in action. After their discipline, "more and more men and women believed in the Lord and were added to their number" (Acts 5:14). For the sake of obedience, renewal, and growth, discipline needs to be lovingly practiced.

Putting Backbone Back in the Church

Church discipline needs to start with two simple programs: church membership and small-group ministries. The church that desires to minimize the need for discipline should not overlook these two simple tools. Neither is revolutionary, but both act as platforms for the exercise of discipline and for preventative maintenance.

Church membership takes on a new perspective when placed alongside discipline. It is difficult to have a disciplinary policy without formal church membership. When a Christian joins a group of God's redeemed, he needs to be aware that he is putting himself under the spiritual umbrella of that church's leadership. This encourages mutual accountability for that entire body.

Teaching about church discipline should be part of any new-member curriculum. This avoids surprises and communicates the level of accountability desired by the fellowship. Mutual commitment also aids self-discipline. A formal membership enhanced with training is a great tool in helping prepare for, and ultimately prevent, discipline in the fellowship.

Every church should also have some form of *small-group ministry*, a place where accountability and intimacy, confession and admonition can take place on a regular basis. When this opportunity is available to a congregation, many of the first embers of improper behavior are lovingly handled before they become roaring fires. That is how the Savior wants it done (Matt. 18:15-16). Close accountability keeps every Christian aware of their frailties and gives a loving atmosphere for dealing with weaknesses. A healthy small-group ministry will keep the need for discipline to a minimum.

The Spirit of the Exercise

The attitude of the church toward discipline is more important than the exercise itself. The call to lovingly correct fellow believers is not a militant one. The church is not to bare its teeth, but to see discipline as an opportunity to redefine love, not as the world defines it, but as God defines it.

Discipline is to be administered with sensitivity and gentle patience, the same attitudes the Savior demonstrated to the woman caught in adultery (John 8:1-11). The value of discipline needs to be understood, but the process must always demonstrate the very Spirit of Jesus. A church concerned with the maturity of its people will discipline with gentleness and love, with restoration the main purpose. Humility will be the prevailing attitude, since we are all vulnerable to the same sins.

The church should not forget that she has no authority to make a judgment about the errant brother's eternal destiny. God alone is the ultimate Judge of all men. Also, every disciplinary situation will be different, demanding flexibility and patience. Some may be private, demanding private attention, while others will be public, calling for public disclosure. In every circumstance, we must be consistent and deal fairly with both the great and small wrongs. Both deep wounds and light scratches must be handled with love. The church's well-being is at stake.

Some day, maybe soon, Christ will return, bringing with him the new heavens and the new earth, and removing the fear of aftershock forever. Until then, may the Savior's people have the courage to love each other properly and place our light back in a dark world. May our commitment return integrity to the church, the most significant force on earth.

> To him who is able to keep you from falling and to present you before his glorious presence without fault and with great joy—to the only God our Savior be glory, majesty, power and authority, through Jesus Christ our Lord, before all ages, now and forevermore! Amen
>
> (Jude 24-25).

Notes

1. Winthrop Hudson, *The Great Tradition of the American Churches* (Edinburgh: T & T. Clark, 1944), 18.

2. Carl Laney, *A Guide to Church Discipline* (Minneapolis: Bethany House Publishers, 1985), 140ff.

Guidelines for the Proper Exercise of Church Discipline

1. Instruct and prepare the church body and the leadership.
   a. The church's position on discipline should be stated in the constitution or other official documents.
   b. The doctrine should be taught in new member classes or in Bible study hour on an annual basis.
   c. The pastor should preach on the subject periodically.
   d. Some churches have members sign statements of commitment to the doctrinal positions and the leadership of the church.

   This step is preliminary to the proper exercise of

discipline and should be an ongoing process.

2. The church should understand God's purposes for the exercise of corrective discipline (see chapter 5), and understand that it must be done in faith.

3. Be sure the offense is "discipline worthy!" Does the offense fall within the guidelines given by the New Testament? Does the sin violate Christian law, unity, love, or truth? (See chapter 10.)

    a. If the sin *is* discipline-worthy, is the wrongdoer a member of the church?

    b. If he is not, is his sin causing contamination of the body?

This step helps to establish whether the offender has committed a sin that demands discipline and, if so, whether the leadership and fellowship are responsible to pursue the actions or to call in another fellowship. If the offender's sin is contaminating the church, contact is necessary *even if* the offender is not a church member.

4. Is the sin public or private? This reveals at what level the discipline process should begin. Private sins call for step one described below; public sins may call for the discipline to begin at step two or three, such as is seen in 1 Corinthians 5:1-5.

5. *Step one* (Matt. 18:15). A face-to-face contact establishing guilt or innocence is essential. Thorough investigation of the charges is necessary.

6. *Step two* (Matt. 18:16). The appeal is to be widened through other brothers as witnesses.

The steps need to be repeated as long as the wrongdoer shows openness to listen and consider the gravity of his sin. Love demands that more than one meeting may be necessary, with sufficient time and prayer between steps.

7. *Step three* (Matt. 18:17a). Communicate the problem to the church leadership.

  a. The leaders should contact the offender to communicate that the matter has moved to a more public level.

  b. The leaders should establish a prayer thrust among themselves and possibly among some of the congregation. A day of prayer and fasting, asking God's direction and involvement, could be considered.

  c. The leaders should plan to involve the entire membership over a period of time. The objective is to slowly and lovingly widen the circle. A "shunning exercise" might be necessary.

  d. The leaders should be clear about both spiritual and legal dangers.

8. *Step four* (Matt. 18:17b). Remove from the offender all membership responsibilities and privileges. The brother is to be treated as a non-Christian. This step is a formal exercise done first by the leaders of the church. The offender should be notified by one of the leaders that this step is being taken.

9. The members should be notified in a private meeting called by the leaders or by confidential letter (to be destroyed) that they are not to fellowship with the offender until repentance is demonstrated.

  a. The discussion of the errant brother's sin should not be done in an open worship service. Safeguarding the integrity and privacy of the fellowship is very important. Order and decency is critical.

  b. Only members are to be allowed in the discussion meetings.

c. Clear biblical instructions should be given as to how to treat the sinner and only the necessary facts about the offense should be communicated. The members should be instructed to keep the matter silent while they withdraw their fellowship and view the offender as a non-Christian in need of evangelism and a relationship with Christ. The church should communicate this message to the offender:

"We find your present conduct unacceptable to God and this congregation. Our love for you therefore demands that we take action which, though painful, we hope by God's grace will result in your repentance and restoration to us."

d. The congregation should never treat the offender with indifference or abhorrence. Jesus was a friend of publicans and sinners, and he manifested concern even for gentiles (nonbelievers).

10. Be watchful and hopeful for the offender to restore his walk with Christ and his relationship to Christ's body.

a. The congregation should mourn and weep over the loss.

b. The membership should wait prayerfully and expectantly for signs of repentance, and be prepared to restore and embrace the brother if repentance comes (2 Cor. 2:7-11). Visible evidence of forgiveness and full restoration is essential on the part of all those who have participated in the process. Ephesians 4:32 must be obeyed: "Be kind and compassionate to one another, forgiving each other, just as in Christ God forgave you."

c. What should be done if you doubt the offender's repentance?

We are not to be judges of hearts, only of behavior. On the other hand, we are not obliged to accept every claim of repentance without questions. When discipline has gone beyond private admonition and has come to involve the church leaders or the whole assembly, some caution should be exercised before total restoration. The repentant offender may be questioned to gain reassurance that his repentance is sincere. The leaders must be careful to prove themselves as wise as serpents but as gentle as doves. In cases where the entire assembly is involved in the proceedings, any members who have factual knowledge adverse to the restoration of the offender should make that information known.

The church and its officers are exercising proper caution when they question applicants for membership before admitting them. In like manner, they are within proper bounds to judiciously and graciously question a disciplined member before full restoration. This would be the case under any of the modes of discipline.

d. Take courage and remember the authority Christ has given to the church to discipline on the earth (Matt. 18:18-20).